MODERN BAND METHOD

Keyboard
Book 1

Scott Burstein
Spencer Hale
Mary Claxton
Dave Wish

Contributors:
Tony Sauza, Clayton McIntyre, Lauren Brown, Joe Panganiban

To access audio and video visit:
www.halleonard.com/mylibrary

Enter Code
4031-9042-2686-0771

ISBN 978-1-5400-7671-7

Visit Hal Leonard Online at
www.halleonard.com

Contact us:
Hal Leonard
7777 West Bluemound Road
Milwaukee, WI 53213
Email: info@halleonard.com

In Europe, contact:
Hal Leonard Europe Limited
1 Red Place
London, W1K 6PL
Email: info@halleonardeurope.com

In Australia, contact:
Hal Leonard Australia Pty. Ltd.
4 Lentara Court
Cheltenham, Victoria, 3192 Australia
Email: info@halleonard.com.au

Introduction

Welcome!

If you are reading this, you have already made the decision to learn to play keyboard so you can play some of your favorite songs. One of the best things about playing in a Modern Band is that you don't need much time to start jammin', but there are also plenty of skills to learn and master over time too. This method book is designed to teach you skills to play keyboard and create music in a variety of popular music styles—pop, rock, R&B, funk, hip-hop, and more. Let's get started!

Jam Tracks 🔊 and Video Lessons ▶️

Use the audio Jam Tracks throughout this book to practice the songs and exercises. Also be sure to watch the included video lessons that demonstrate many of the techniques and concepts. To access all of the audio and video files for download or streaming, just visit *www.halleonard.com/mylibrary* and enter the code found on page 1 of this book.

The Keyboard

Sound/Volume controls

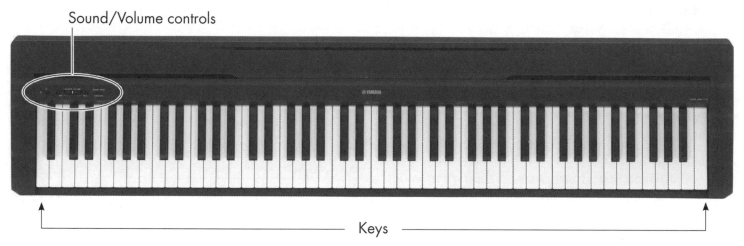

Keys

Some keyboards come with simple controls that allow you to increase and decrease your overall volume. Others are more complex, with several buttons, knobs, dials, and switches that allow you to shape the tone of the instrument. In this book, you only need to use a basic, natural sound of a real piano. However, if you happen to have a keyboard with several options to work with, then feel free to experiment in the songs throughout the book!

Basic Technique ▶

You can sit or stand to play the keyboard. The keyboard stand and bench (if you're sitting) should be adjusted for your height.

The musical alphabet uses seven different letters, from A to G, and then repeats. You can easily find these on the white keys of our keyboard. On the keyboard, we have consistent numbers for the fingers:

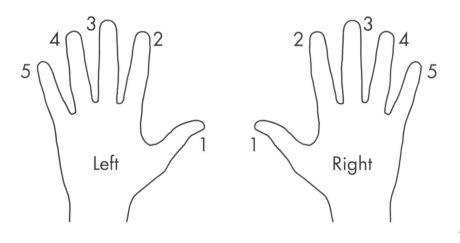

Iconic Notation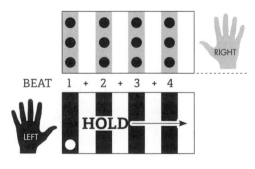

Here are a few graphics that will show up throughout each section. The first is a chord diagram showing the white and black keys. The keys that are shaded in are the keys that should be played to perform the labeled chord. You can press down at the same time to play a full chord or play them in different combinations to create various **comping** patterns (improvised rhythmic accompaniment to a melody), which we will discuss later in the book. This first graphic is the E minor (Emi) chord. The numbers below each shaded key refer to your finger numbers:

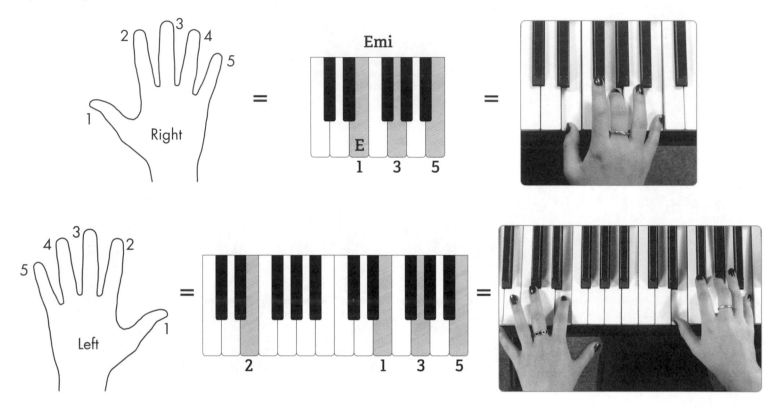

Rhythms in **iconic notation** are read left to right. All of the music used in this book is counted in groups of four. Count these numbers steadily ("1 + 2 + 3 + 4 + "). The "+" sign stands for the word "and." The black dots represent the three notes of the chord. The white dot represents a single bass note.

In the case of the Emi chord, for example, your right hand would play all three notes on every beat while your left hand only plays the note E on beat 1.

This iconic notation will aid you in your comping. **Comping** means using your musical knowledge to make up rhythms over a chord progression that fits a song's style. Throughout this book, we will give examples of these rhythms to increase your comping vocabulary.

This book is designed for you to learn alongside other Modern Band musicians so you can jam with your friends and classmates, but it can also be used as a stand-alone book to learn to play the keyboard. Though some of the skills that you will be working on during each section will be different from those of the other instruments, all of the Full Band Songs 🎸 are designed to be played by a whole band together. Now it's time to start playing some music!

SECTION 1

Playing Chords: One-Chord Jam and Adding Bass Notes

Play the Emi chord with your right hand using the rhythms below (1, 2, and 3), and play the bass note E with your left hand.

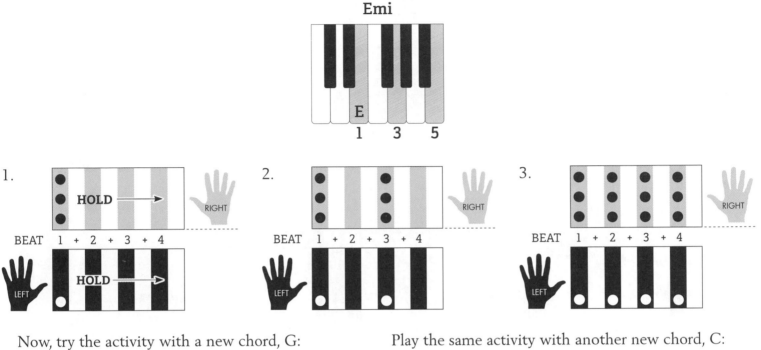

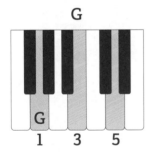

Now, try the activity with a new chord, G:

Play the same activity with another new chord, C:

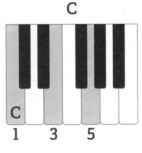

Notice that all of these chords have the same shape: three notes on the white keys with a skipped note between each finger.

Improvisation: Two-Note Solo

These two notes, E and G, can be used to take a solo. Unlike the chord diagrams, this image shows two notes that you can play on the keyboard, one after the other:

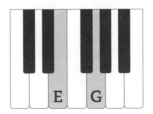

Practice playing these two notes in a variety of ways by mixing up the rhythm and order. Here are some ideas for improvisation:

- Start by playing the E twice and then switching to the G.
- Alternate between the two notes rapidly and then slowly. Then, try changing speeds.
- Focus on creating distinct rhythms and lock in with the Jam Track.
- Play a rhythm on just the E, and then repeat that rhythm on the G.

Music Theory: The Song Chart

The most common way popular music is written is in the form of a **lead sheet**, which is a type of **song chart**. A lead sheet is broken into **measures** (or **bars**) which are divided by thick vertical lines. The dashes between those lines represent beats of music. This song has four beats per measure because there are four **slashes** (/) between each vertical line. The signs at the beginning and end of the example are called **repeat bars**; the two dots mean to repeat those chords in those measures over and over again.

The next part of the lead sheet is the chords.

This song plays a G chord for four beats (one measure), then an Emi chord for four beats, a C chord for four beats, and then another Emi chord again for four beats.

CAN'T STOP THE FEELING!

Justin Timberlake

Another way music is written is writing the names of chords over the lyrics. This chart doesn't tell you how many beats to play each chord, but it shows you which lyrics to sing when the chords change. Play G when you sing "feeling" and switch to Emi on the word "bones."

     G   **Emi**
I've got this feeling inside my bones.

     C   **Emi**
It goes electric, wavy when I turn it on.

     G   **Emi**
All through my city, all through my home,

     C   **Emi**
We're flying up, no ceiling, when we in our zone.

     G   **Emi**
I got that sunshine in my pocket, got that good soul in my feet.

     C   **Emi**
I feel that hot blood in my body when it drops, ooh.

     G   **Emi**
I can't take my eyes up off it, moving so phenomenally.

     C   **Emi**
Room on lock the way we rock it, so don't stop.

Here are some other songs that use these three chords: Emi, G, and C.

WITHOUT YOU
David Guetta ft. Usher

G
I can't win, I can't reign. I will never win this game **C** without you, **Emi** without you. **C**

G
I am lost, I am vain. I will never be the same **C** without you, **Emi** without you. **C**

G
I won't run, I won't fly. I will never make it by **C** without you, **Emi** without you. **C**

G
I can't rest, I can't fight. All I need is you and I, **C** without you, **Emi** without you. **C**

SEND MY LOVE (TO YOUR NEW LOVER)
Adele

G
This was all you, none of it me. You put your hands on, on my body and told me, **Emi**
you told me you were ready

G
For the big one, for the big jump. I'd be your last love, everlasting, you and me. **Emi**
That was what you told me.

G
I'm giving you up, I've forgiven it all. You set me free. **Emi**

G
Send my love to your new lover, treat her better.

Emi
We've gotta let go of all of our ghosts. We both know we ain't kids no more.

G
Send my love to your new lover, treat her better.

Emi
We've gotta let go of all of our ghosts.
We both know we ain't kids no more.

In this next chart, the first two chords last two beats each while the chord that follows last for four beats.

WAKE ME UP
Avicii ft. John Legend

Emi   **C**   **G**
Feeling my way through the darkness,

Emi   **C**   **G**
Guided by a beating heart.

Emi   **C**   **G**
I can't tell where the journey will end,

Emi **C**   **G**
But I know where to start.

Emi   **C**   **G**
They tell me I'm too young to understand.

Emi   **C**   **G**
They say I'm caught up in a dream.

Emi   **C**   **G**
Well, life will pass me by if I don't open up my eyes.

Emi   **C**   **G**
Well, that's fine by me.

          Emi   **C**   **G**
So wake me up when it's all over,

          Emi **C**   **G**
When I'm wiser and I'm older.

          Emi   **C**   **G**
All this time I was finding myself

          Emi   **C**   **G**
And I didn't know I was lost.

Composition: C, Emi, and G

Compose (write) a progression using the Emi, G, and C chords with any of the comping patterns you have used so far. Place them in the song chart grid below to create a new song:

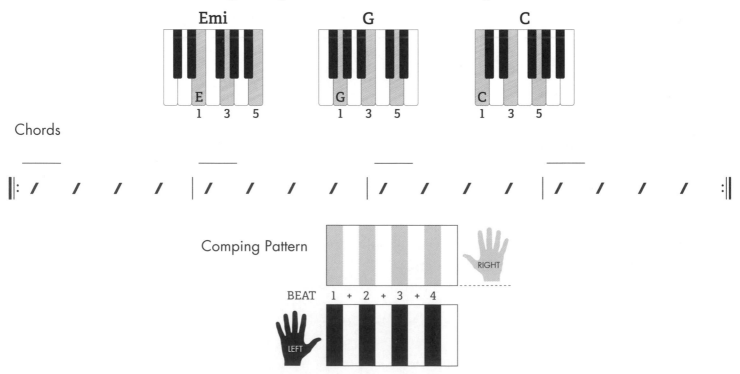

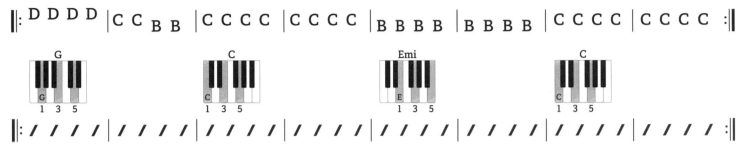

Full Band Song: I GOTTA FEELING

The Black Eyed Peas

Form of Recording: Intro–Chorus–Verse–Chorus–Verse–Chorus

In this song, we introduce **melodic notation** for the keyboard. Melodic notation is used to show melodies with single notes rather than chords. Each letter means to play that note once. The letters move up and down to show you whether to move up (to the right) or down (to the left) on the keyboard.

‖: D D D D │ C C B B │ C C C C │ C C C C │ B B B B │ B B B B │ C C C C │ C C C C :‖

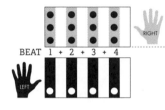

‖: / / / / │ / / / / │ / / / / │ / / / / │ / / / / │ / / / / │ / / / / │ / / / / :‖

Use this rhythm for the Chorus:

And this rhythm for the Verse:

You can use these notes to take a solo in this song:

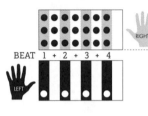

CHORUS

G   **C**
I gotta feeling that tonight's gonna be a good night,

                Emi   **C**
That tonight's gonna be a good night, that tonight's gonna be a good, good night.

VERSE

G   **C**
Tonight's the night, let's live it up. I got my money, let's spend it up.

Emi   **C**
Go out and smash it, like, oh my God. Jump off that sofa, let's get, get off.

VERSE

G   **C**
I know that we'll have a ball if we get down and go out and just lose it all.

      Emi   **C**
I feel stressed out, I wanna let go. Let's go way out, spaced out, and losing all control.

VERSE

G   **C**
Fill up my cup, Mazel Tov! Look at her dancing, just take it off.

Emi
Let's paint the town, we'll shut it down.
     C
Let's burn the roof, and then we'll do it again.

Going Beyond: Singing and Playing

An important skill for a popular musician is to not only play songs, but also to sing along. Here are a few tips for singing and playing:

- Make sure you have the keyboard part down well enough that you can play it without thinking about changing chords, and then try speaking the lyrics (in rhythm) over it.
- Sing the lyrics while playing the chords with just the right hand. Only move your hand when it's time to change chords.
- Don't worry too much about singing the correct pitches (notes) at this point; just practice the skill of doing two things at once.

Playing Chords: One-Chord Song 🔊

It's time to learn a new chord! This chord, A, uses a black key in addition to two white keys. Use the diagram to learn it, and then try it with the rhythm pattern below to play "Low Rider" by War.

LOW RIDER 🔊
War

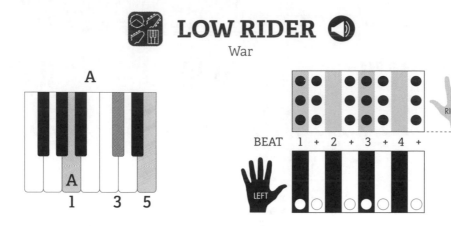

You can also practice a different two-note solo:

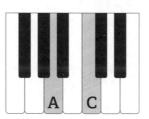

Music Theory: Naming the Black Keys ▶️

Play the note C. Now play one black key to the *right*. This note is C-sharp (C♯). To name a black key, add "sharp" (♯) to the name of the white key just to its left.

Play the note D. Go one black key to the *left*. This note is D-flat (D♭). To name a black key, you can also add "flat" (♭) to the name of the white key just to its right.

Therefore, each black key has two names. C♯ and D♭ are the same note, but they have different names:

Now that you know some new notes, you can play this riff:

DARK HORSE 🔊
Katy Perry

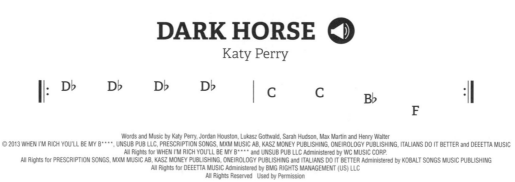

‖: D♭   D♭   D♭   D♭ | C   C   B♭   :‖
                                                 F

Some songs are based on chords, some on riffs, and some use both.

Here is another riff that sounds best when played with the lower notes of the keyboard:

25 OR 6 TO 4
Chicago

‖: A A A A A | G G G G G | G♭ G♭ G♭ G♭ G♭ | F F F F E E E E :‖

Which fingerings work best for this riff? Since you are playing five different notes, you can use all five fingers. Start with your left-hand thumb (1) on A and your pinky (5) on E.

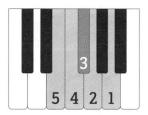

Instrument Technique: Balancing the Fingers

It's important that your fingers are equally as strong to play all types of music. To help get you there, you can play the following exercises starting with just one hand at a time and then together:

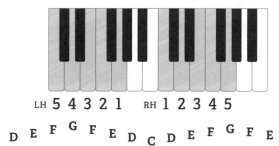 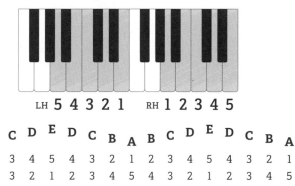

LH 5 4 3 2 1   RH 1 2 3 4 5   LH 5 4 3 2 1   RH 1 2 3 4 5

| | | | G | F | | | | | | | | | G | F | | | | | | | | | D | | | | | | | | | D | | | | |
| C | D | E | | | E | D | C | D | E | F | | | F | E | D | C | | A | B | C | | | D | C | B | A | B | C | | | D | C | B | A |

RH 1 2 3 4 5 4 3 2 1 2 3 4 5 4 3 2 1   RH 1 2 3 4 5 4 3 2 1 2 3 4 5 4 3 2 1
LH 5 4 3 2 1 2 3 4 5 4 3 2 1 2 3 4 5   LH 5 4 3 2 1 2 3 4 5 4 3 2 1 2 3 4 5

Begin slowly, and then speed up. Go back and forth until you can play each note clearly.

Music Theory: Minor vs. Major

Compare the Ami and A chord. What is different?

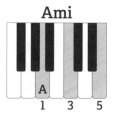   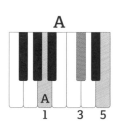

What is the difference in sound? How would you describe it?

The A chord's full name is really "A major" (it's assumed that a chord is a major chord unless told otherwise). All major chords have a similar quality of sound, and all minor chords do, too. Moving between them is always the same: the middle note moves one key to the left to go from major to minor.

Try playing a bar of each chord using these suggested rhythm:

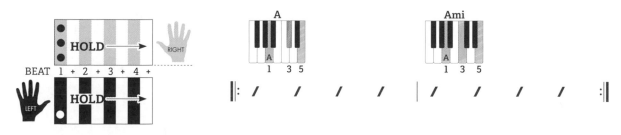

Here is another song where you can practice moving from a major chord to a minor chord:

SHOUT
The Isley Brothers

Improvisation: Four-Note Solo

Improvise with these four notes:

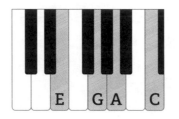

You can try lots of fingerings here based on which notes you are using for your solo. For instance, if you want to use all four notes in a row, then try playing E with 1, G with 2, A with 3, and C with 5, all with the right hand. However, if you want to alternate quickly between the A and C and then move down to E and G, you might use 1 and 3 for both and move your hand up and down the range of the keys.

Music Theory: Whole Notes and Half Notes

So far in each measure of our music, you have counted four beats. A single note played for four beats is called a **whole note**. If you cut it in half, it becomes two **half notes**. Each whole note is four beats long and each half note is two beats long.

Below are how whole notes and half notes appear in both iconic rhythmic notation and traditional **staff notation**:

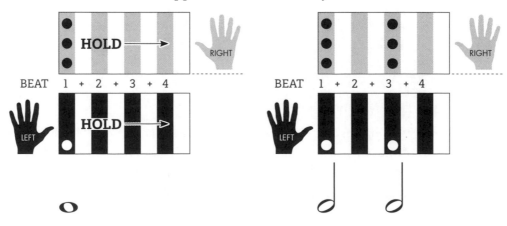

Using everything you have learned in this section (sharps, flats, half and whole notes), you can play through the Verse and Chorus of "Heathens" by Twenty One Pilots.

Form of Recording: Chorus–Verse–Chorus–Verse–Chorus–Chorus

Using the chord diagrams and staff notation provided, you can play the Verse and Chorus of the second Full Band Song! This song has new chords in it. Use the diagrams to learn which notes to play for each:

For many Modern Band charts, the keyboard player has many options for what they can play. They can play the chords, the melody, a bass line, or a combination of all of these. Do what works best for you.

Melody Phrase 1

$|^B{}^C_B{}^B{}^C_B{}_G|_E$ $|^B{}^C_B{}^B{}^C_B{}_G|_E$

Melody Phrase 2

$\|{}^E|_D{}_C{}^E_D{}_C{}^E|^E{}_B$ $|{}^E_D{}_C{}^E_D{}_C{}^E|^E{}_B\|$

The only other part of the song that is different from this is the last two bars of every Verse. This chord looks different than previous chords, but you can use your knowledge of the chord diagrams to play it.

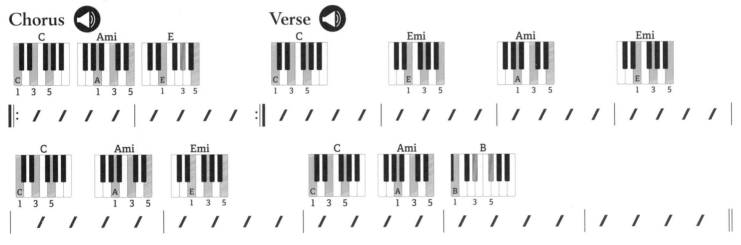

CHORUS

C   Ami   E   C   Ami   E
All my friends are heathens, take it slow. Wait for them to ask you who you know.

        C   Ami   E   C   Ami   E
Please don't make any sudden moves. You don't know the half of the abuse.

VERSE

C
Welcome to the room of people who have rooms of people
              Emi
        that they loved one day docked away.

Ami
Just because we check the guns at the door doesn't mean
        Emi
        our brains will change from hand grenades.

C   Ami   Emi
You'll never know the psychopath sitting next to you.
        You'll never know the murderer sitting next to you.

C   Ami   B
You'll think, "How'd I get here, sitting next to you?"
        But after all I've said, please don't forget.

SECTION 3

Instrument Technique: Separate Hands

To play this next riff, line up your hands in two different places on the keyboard, keeping space between them. Shift your pinky finger from the G note to D between the measures. The darkened keys below are the ones you'll need to play this riff (listen to the original recording to determine the rhythm):

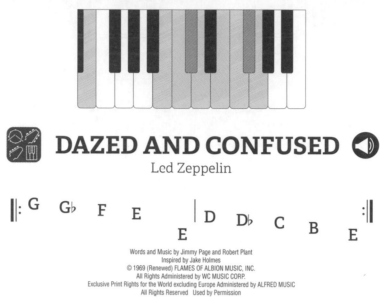

🎹 DAZED AND CONFUSED 🔊
Led Zeppelin

‖: G G♭ F E | D D♭ C B :‖
              E   E

Playing Chords: The D Chord

When you combine the D chord with the A chord, you can play a variety of songs. Try playing these two chords with both your right and left hands. Here are a few songs to practice playing the new chord:

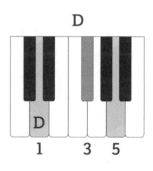

🎹 IMAGINE 🔊
John Lennon

In this first example, the notes in the comping pattern are "broken." This means that you must play the top two notes of the chord, and then the bottom note, alternating back and forth.

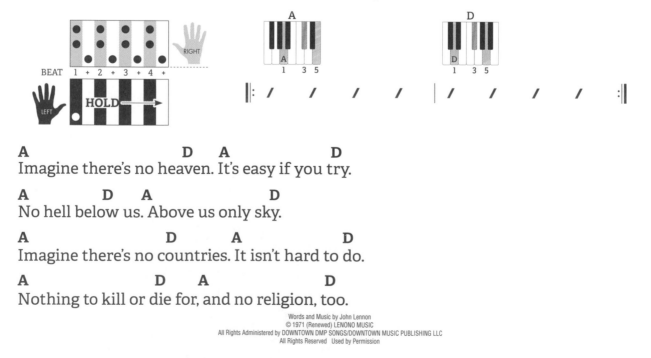

A   D   A   D
Imagine there's no heaven. It's easy if you try.

A   D   A   D
No hell below us. Above us only sky.

A   D   A   D
Imagine there's no countries. It isn't hard to do.

A   D   A   D
Nothing to kill or die for, and no religion, too.

BEST DAY OF MY LIFE

American Authors

Notice that the left hand and right hand play different rhythms here. Practice them separately, and then together.

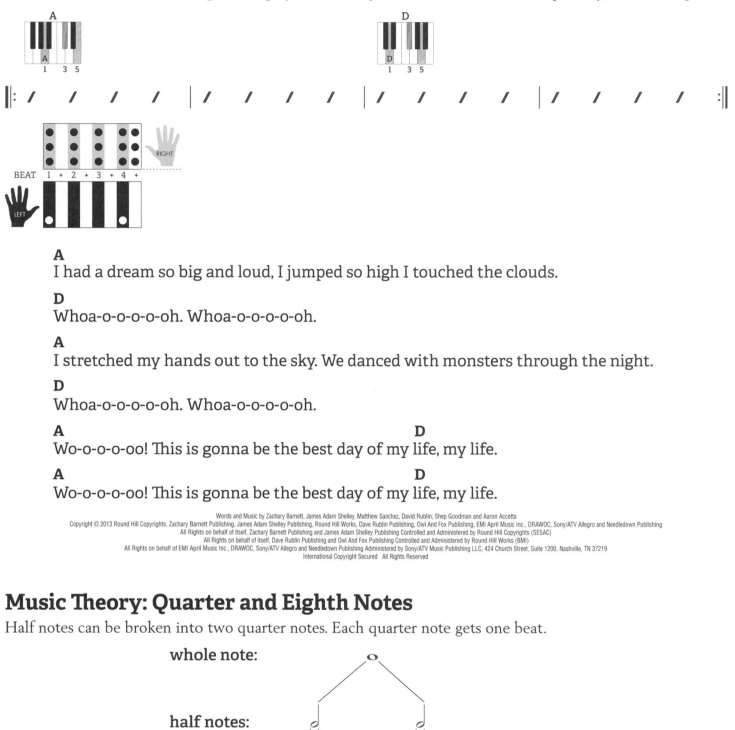

A
I had a dream so big and loud, I jumped so high I touched the clouds.

D
Whoa-o-o-o-o-oh. Whoa-o-o-o-o-oh.

A
I stretched my hands out to the sky. We danced with monsters through the night.

D
Whoa-o-o-o-o-oh. Whoa-o-o-o-o-oh.

A   **D**
Wo-o-o-o-oo! This is gonna be the best day of my life, my life.

A   **D**
Wo-o-o-o-oo! This is gonna be the best day of my life, my life.

Music Theory: Quarter and Eighth Notes

Half notes can be broken into two quarter notes. Each quarter note gets one beat.

whole note:

half notes:

quarter notes:

This comping pattern uses only quarter notes:

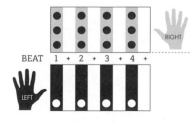

Here is the same pattern in standard rhythmic notation:

17

Playing and Resting a Chord ▶

You can also use a quarter rest when you want to stop the chord and leave some space. Try this on the A chord:

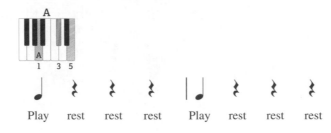

Play   rest   rest   rest   Play   rest   rest   rest

You can use a **half rest** to take the place of two quarter rests: ━

Sometimes, you'll see a symbol called a **whole rest**; it's used to let you know when no notes or chords will be played for the entire measure: ▬

This comping pattern is useful to practice when changing chords:

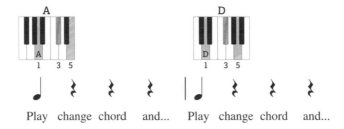

Play   change   chord   and...   Play   change   chord   and...

Quarter notes can be broken into eighth notes. Each note gets half a beat.

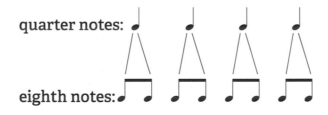

quarter notes:

eighth notes:

This represents a full measure of eighth notes:

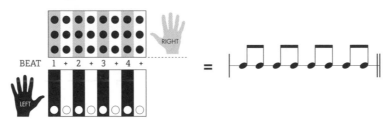

These rhythms combine quarter notes with eighth notes. Try counting along as you play:

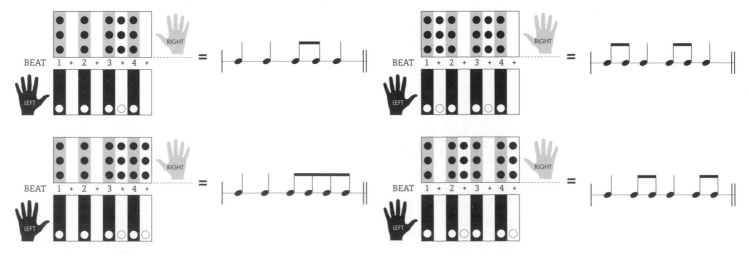

Improvisation: The Major Pentatonic Scale ▶

The Jam Card is a tool you can use to learn chords and scales on the keyboard. There are many Jam Cards in the Modern Band Method, but we've only included a handful of them in Book 1. Locate Jam Card #4a, which looks like a piano keyboard with different, shaded vertical bars. Then, place the card behind the keys of the keyboard, lining the root bars up with the note A.

This Jam Card shows you which notes are used in the major pentatonic scale. Use the gray notes to play the complete scale and solo. You can practice improvising over the Jam Track.

Composition: Composing a Riff ▶

Here are some sample riffs, with rhythms underneath. Practice them first by playing each measure separately, and then play them all together. These use only the notes highlighted by the Jam Card.

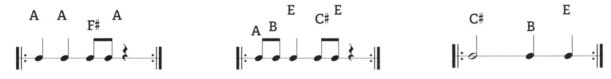

Write your original two-bar riff here; you can use the Jam Card as a reference if you'd like:

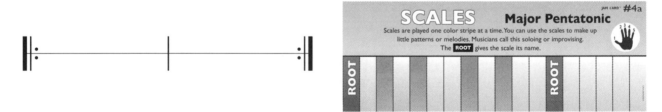

You can play your composed riff over the A-to-D chord progression. Here are some new comping patterns you can use:

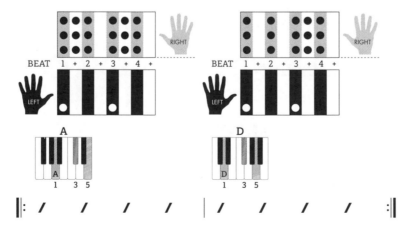

SECTION 4

Instrument Technique: Learning New Riffs

KIDS
MGMT

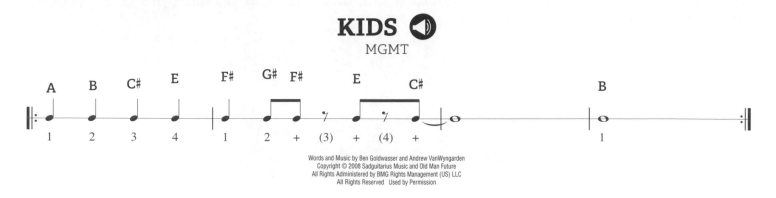

In the second measure of the example above, the melody has several notes that land on the upbeats (the "+" between the beats). This is called a **syncopated rhythm**. **Syncopation** is when there is an accent on the upbeats. "Take on Me" by aha has a melody that rises up and descends down a scale with syncopation:

TAKE ON ME
aha

Playing Chords: Chord Review and New Songs

You played the E chord in "Heathens":

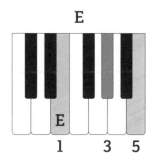

Here are some more songs that use the E chord:

WE WILL ROCK YOU
Queen

In these next two songs, you'll play some rhythms starting on downbeats and others on upbeats. Listen to the Jam Tracks if you need help counting the rhythms.

Composition: Writing Lyrics

Here are three steps you can take to help you write lyrics:
- Pick a theme—lyrics can be easy to write when you have something you want to say. Think of something you care about and write based on that, such as friends, family, hobbies, or dreams.
- Choose two words that rhyme, such as "great" and "late" or "thrill" and "chill." Then, choose another pair of words.
- Turn your pairs of words into sentences, and then try to speak the words in rhythm and sing them along with the Jam Track. Here's an example of a verse for a song written about songwriting:

| Writing | lyrics | is | so | fun, | | can | be | done | by | any | - | one. |

| Think | of | what | to | write | a - | bout; | | play | some | chords, | and | sing | or | shout! |

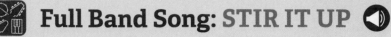

Full Band Song: STIR IT UP

Bob Marley & the Wailers

Form of Recording: Intro–Chorus–Verse–Chorus–Verse–Chorus

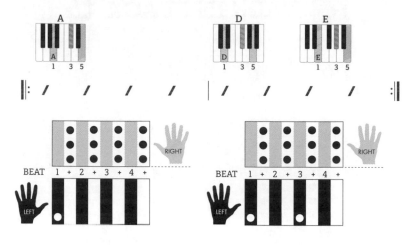

Improvisation Scale

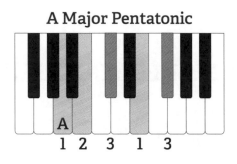

A Major Pentatonic

CHORUS

A   D   E   A   D   E
Stir it up. Little darlin', stir it up. Come on, baby.

             A   D   E A   D   E
Come on and stir it up. Little darlin', stir it up. O-oh!

VERSE

    A   D
It's been a long, long time, yeah (stir it, stir it, stir it together).

E   A   D   E
Since I got you on my mind (ooh-ooh-ooh-ooh).

A   D   E
Now you are here (stir it, stir it, stir it together). I said, it's so clear.

    A   D   E
To see what we could do, baby (ooh-ooh-ooh-ooh). Just me and you.

SECTION 5

Instrument Technique: Arpeggios ▶

Another way you can play chords is by playing **arpeggios**. Instead of playing all the notes at once, split the chord up, playing each note one at a time. Here are three ways you might arpeggiate new chords:

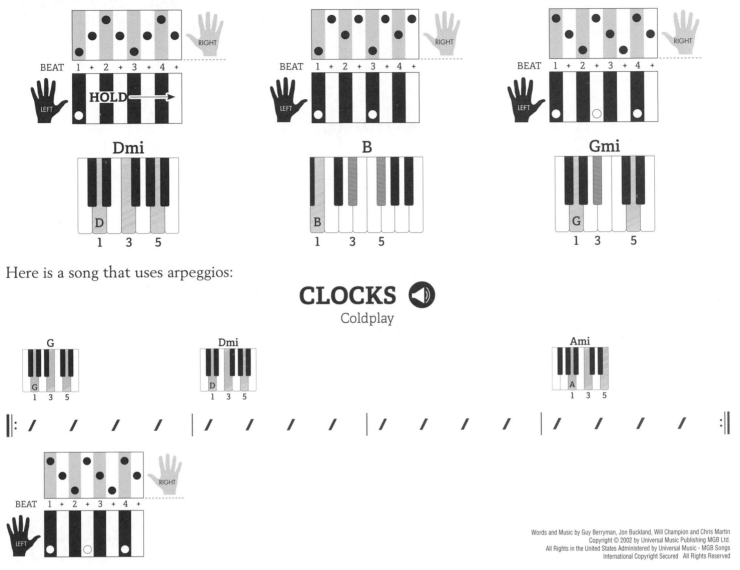

Here is a song that uses arpeggios:

CLOCKS 🔊
Coldplay

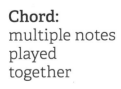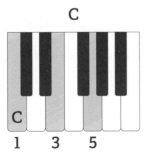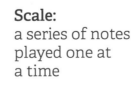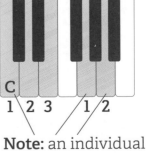

Music Theory: Notes, Chords, and Scales

All music is made up of the notes of the musical alphabet. All the riffs and chords you have been playing are made up these individual notes. There are seven natural notes: A–B–C–D–E–F–G.

Chords are a combination of notes played together. The chords you've played are each made of three notes.

Chord: multiple notes played together

Scale: a series of notes played one at a time

Note: an individual pitch or sound that makes up music

A **scale** is a series of notes. The collection of notes we've been using to solo is an example of a scale. The combination of notes, chords, and scales put to rhythms creates all the music we experience.

23

Improvisation: The Full Minor Pentatonic ▶

The next scale is the **minor pentatonic scale**. If you place the root bar of Jam Card #4b on A, then you can play an A minor pentatonic scale with the notes A, C, D, E, and G.

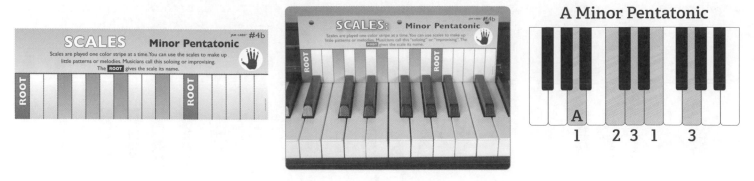

How is this different from the **major pentatonic scale**? What are the different notes? How does it sound different?

This scale can be played with songs that are in the **key** (a collection of notes that form the basis of a song) of A minor or have a bluesy or funky sound, such as "Low Rider" by War. Since this scale spans a lot of space on the keyboard, you'll need to shift your hand. Here are a few different melodic ideas that show you how to shift your fingers:

Stepwise and Skipping Motion ▶

Stepwise motion:

A C D C D E D E G E G A
1 2 3 1 2 3 1 2 3 1 2 3

Skipping motion:

A D C E D G E A
1 3 1 3 1 4 1 4

Here are some riffs that use the pentatonic scale:

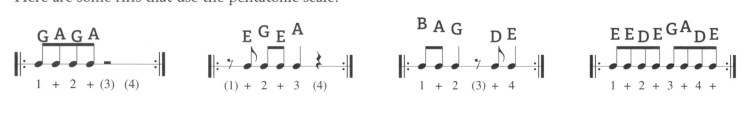

G A G A
1 + 2 + (3) (4)

E G E A
(1) + 2 + 3 (4)

B A G D E
1 + 2 (3) + 4

E E D E G A D E
1 + 2 + 3 + 4 +

Now, try composing your own riff:

SECTION 6

LAND OF A THOUSAND DANCES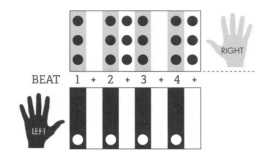
Wilson Pickett

When playing this one-chord song, listen carefully to your bandmates or the Jam Track to make sure you're locking in with the groove:

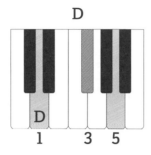

Instrument Technique: Phrasing—Legato and Staccato

One of the best ways to create interest with very few notes is with **phrasing** and **articulation**, particularly how long and connected (**legato**) or separated and short (**staccato**) you play a note.

In music, when there is a **slur** or **tenuto** marking over or under a series of notes, play them smoothly:

Slur

Tenuto marking

When there is a dot included with one or multiple notes, play them staccato:

Here are a few riffs that demonstrate this; listen to each and play them with the appropriate phrasing:

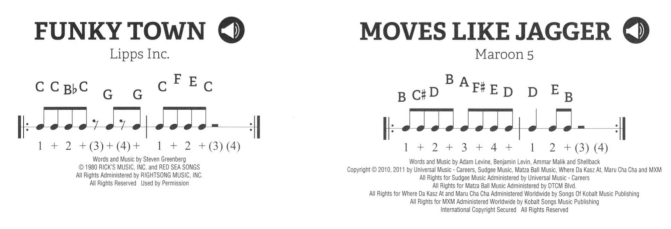

FUNKY TOWN
Lipps Inc.

C C Bb C   G G   C F E C

1 + 2 +(3)+(4)+   1 + 2 +(3)(4)

Words and Music by Steven Greenberg
© 1980 RICK'S MUSIC, INC. and RED SEA SONGS
All Rights Administered by RIGHTSONG MUSIC, INC.
All Rights Reserved   Used by Permission

MOVES LIKE JAGGER
Maroon 5

B C# D B A F# E D D E B

1 + 2 + 3 + 4 +   1 2 +(3)(4)

Words and Music by Adam Levine, Benjamin Levin, Ammar Malik and Shellback
Copyright © 2010, 2011 by Universal Music - Careers, Sudgee Music, Matza Ball Music, Where Da Kasz At, Maru Cha Cha and MXM
All Rights for Sudgee Music Administered by Universal Music - Careers
All Rights for Matza Ball Music Administered by DTCM Blvd.
All Rights for Where Da Kasz At and Maru Cha Cha Administered Worldwide by Songs Of Kobalt Music Publishing
All Rights for MXM Administered Worldwide by Kobalt Songs Music Publishing
International Copyright Secured   All Rights Reserved

Here is a riff that alternates between long and short articulations:

SUMMER
Calvin Harris

G   G G A A B B G   G F# F# E E D D G

Words and Music by Calvin Harris
Copyright © 2014 TSJ Merlyn Licensing B.V.
All Rights Administered by Sony/ATV Music Publishing LLC, 424 Church Street, Suite 1200, Nashville, TN 37219
International Copyright Secured   All Rights Reserved

25

Improvisation: Applying Legato and Staccato

When improvising during the jams, be sure to mix in legato and staccato phrasing. Here are some riffs to try out with legato and staccato articulations:

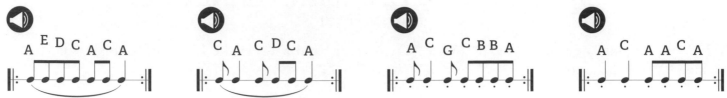

Music Theory: Notes on the Staff

You've learned how to play several melodies so far using letter name notation. But this notation is sometimes not perfectly clear. For instance, which A should you use when there are seven different ones to choose from? This is where **standard staff notation** can be helpful.

To start, look at a familiar melody from a song you have already learned, "Heathens" by Twenty One Pilots. The song begins with the notes B, C, and G, but where do we find them on the piano? Here is where these pitches are located on the keyboard:

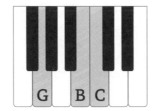

Each note on the keyboard has an exact place it appears on a **music staff**. A music staff has five lines and four spaces, and it looks like this:

The next important feature on a staff is the **clef**. There are quite a few of these in the music world, but for now, we will just use the **treble clef.** Here is what the treble clef looks like on the staff:

You have already seen noteheads in standard staff rhythms. Here, they are placed on the staff in the lines and spaces to let the musician know which notes to play. The notehead's vertical placement determines which specific pitch it is. Here is the vocal melody in staff notation:

Finally, add in the rhythms you learned earlier to show the rhythm in the same place as the notes. In the case of this song, there is a full measure of eighth notes followed by a measure filled entirely by one whole note:

B C B G B C B G   E

Each note corresponds to one of the seven letters of the musical alphabet. While every note name can be found in multiple places, each specific name for the note is only in one place on the staff. Look at the notes on the staff that take us from the bottom line to the top line and their location on the keyboard:

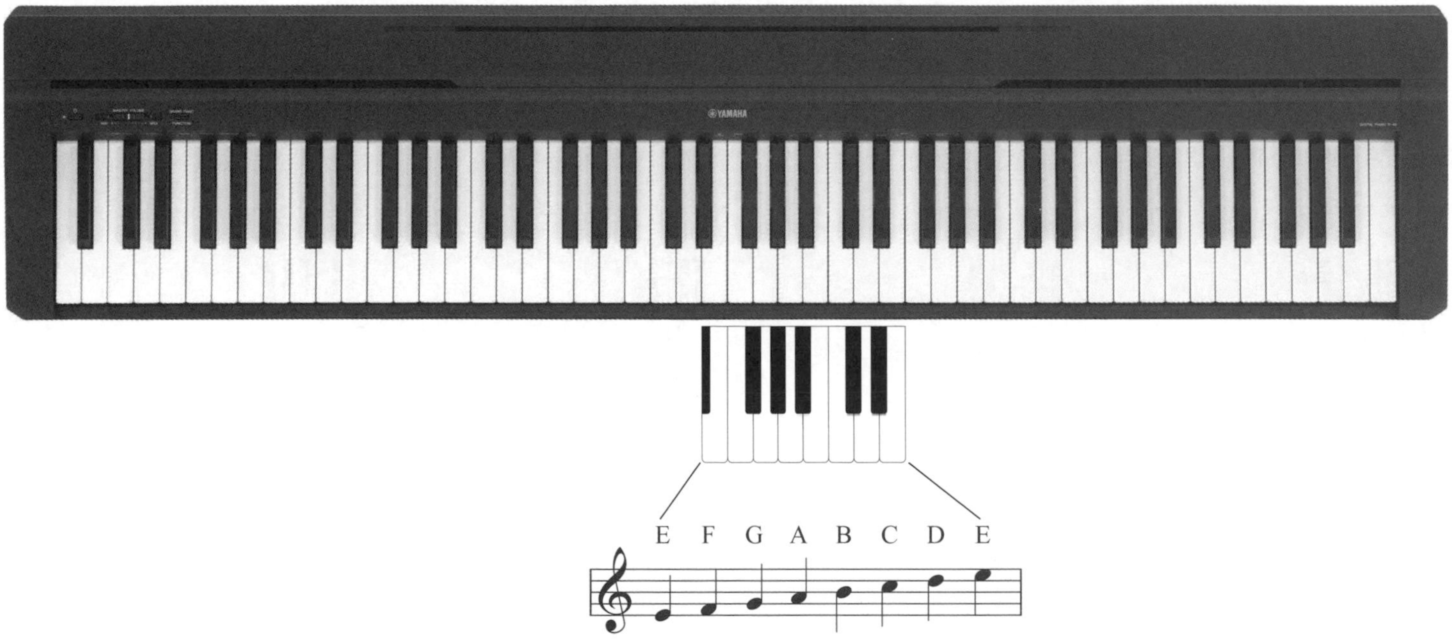

Write the melody in the staff below for the first two measures and the last part of the fourth measure. Then, write the note names over the single-line notes for the third and fourth measures. We have slightly changed the rhythm so it only uses the note values we have discussed so far.

BAD ROMANCE

Lady Gaga

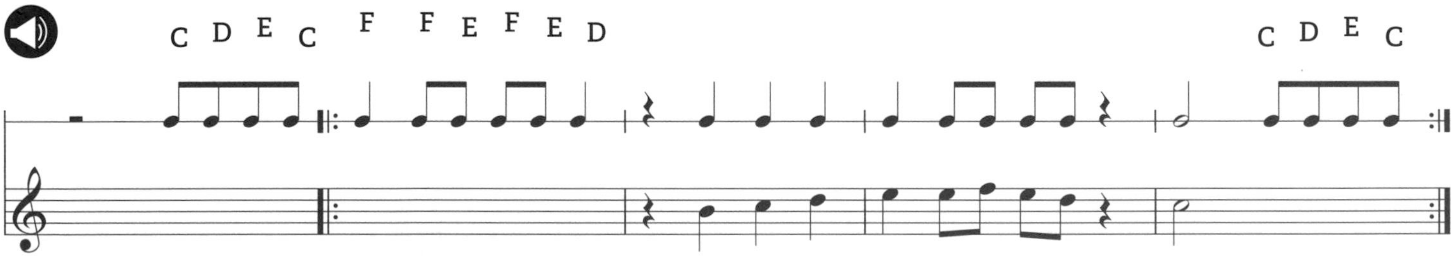

Now, try playing your example by reading the staff notation.

To play the next melody from the song, you'll need to know the **eighth rest:** 𝄾

This rest is the same value as one eighth note. When combined with another eighth note or eighth rest, it makes up a full beat. Listen to a recording of the song to hear the original rhythms. This melody happens at the 0:29 mark:

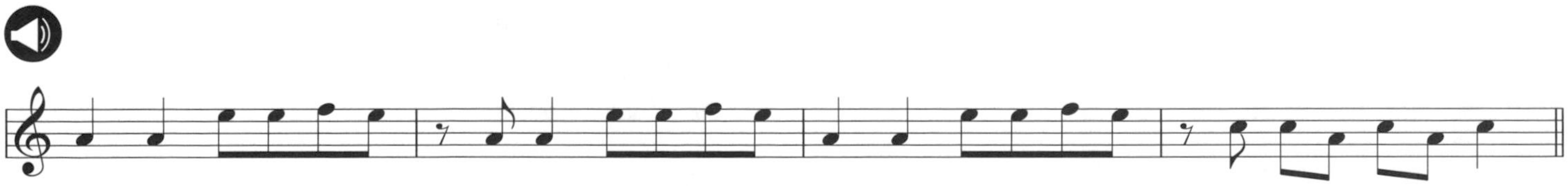

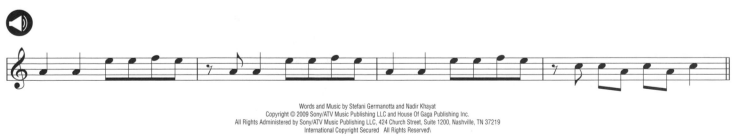

Words and Music by Stefani Germanotta and Nadir Khayat
Copyright © 2009 Sony/ATV Music Publishing LLC and House Of Gaga Publishing Inc.
All Rights Administered by Sony/ATV Music Publishing LLC, 424 Church Street, Suite 1200, Nashville, TN 37219
International Copyright Secured All Rights Reserved\

Adele

Form of Recording: Intro–Verse–Pre-Chorus–Chorus–Verse–Pre-Chorus–Chorus–Bridge–Chorus

This song has a riff with a **sixteenth-note** syncopated rhythm. Sixteenth notes work in a similar way to how eighth notes relate to quarter notes, in that two sixteenth notes are equal to one eighth note. They are counted as: "1–e–+–a," etc.

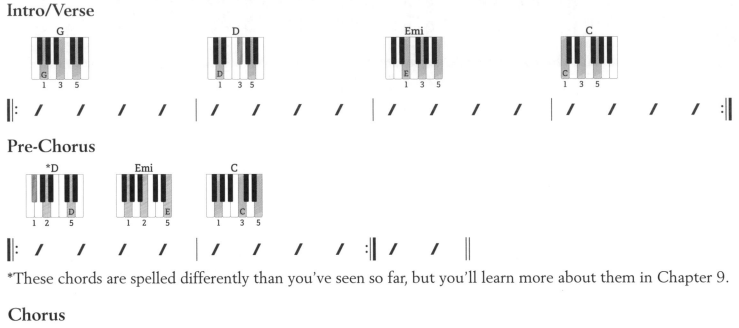

Intro/Verse

Pre-Chorus

*These chords are spelled differently than you've seen so far, but you'll learn more about them in Chapter 9.

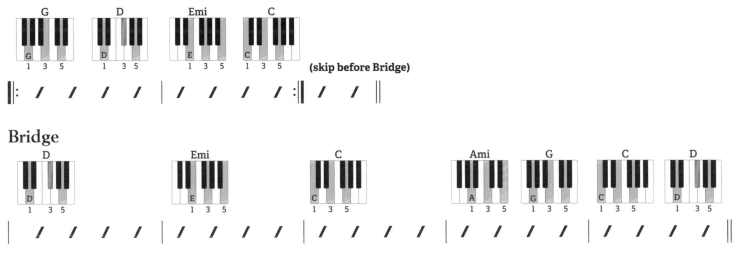

Chorus

(skip before Bridge)

Bridge

You can use this comping pattern over each section of the song:

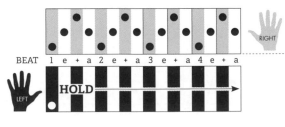

You can also use this scale to solo over the song:

G Major Pentatonic

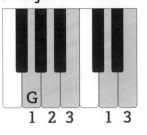

VERSE

G   D   Emi   C
I heard that you're settled down, that you found a girl and you're married now.

G   D   Emi   C
I heard that your dreams came true. Guess she gave you things I didn't give to you.

G   D   Emi   C
Old friend, why are you so shy? Ain't like you to hold back or hide from the light.

PRE-CHORUS

D   Emi   C
I hate to turn up out of the blue uninvited, but I couldn't stay away, I couldn't fight it.

D   Emi   C
I had hoped you'd see my face and that you'd be reminded that for me it isn't over.

CHORUS

G   D   Emi   C
Never mind, I'll find someone like you.

              G   D   Emi   C
I wish nothing but the best for you two.

G   D   Emi   C
Don't forget me, I beg. I'll remember you said,

              G   D   Emi   C
"Sometimes it lasts in love, but sometimes it hurts instead,

              G   D   Emi   C
Sometimes it lasts in love, but sometimes it hurts instead."

BRIDGE

D
Nothing compares, no worries or cares,

      Emi
Regrets and mistakes, they're memories made.

C   Ami   G   C   D
Who would have known how bittersweet this would taste?

SECTION 7

Playing Chords: Various Comping Patterns

Practice playing through these patterns while staying on the chord of your choice. Then, try changing the chord for each pattern:

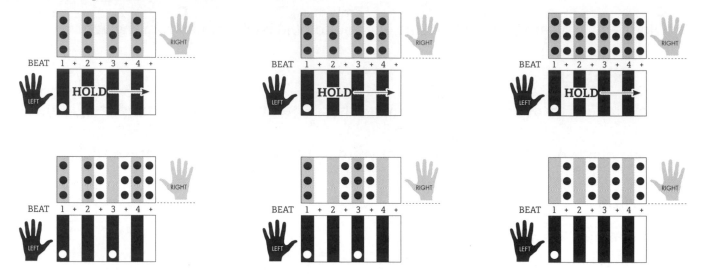

Composition: Introduction

Many songs have an **introduction**. An introduction is often the instrumental section that happens before the vocalist begins to sing. To compose the introduction, write four bars, being sure to use at least one minor chord:

Chords

$$\|: \quad / \quad / \quad / \quad / \quad | \quad / \quad / \quad / \quad / \quad | \quad / \quad / \quad / \quad / \quad | \quad / \quad / \quad / \quad / \quad :\|$$

Comping Pattern

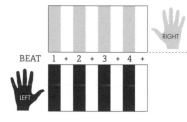

Now, add a riff to your introduction using this scale:

A Minor Pentatonic

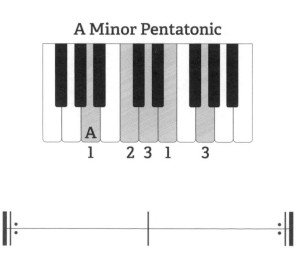

30

Music Theory: Transposition ▶

Now that you are familiar with a variety of chords, you can play songs in any key through a process of **transposition**, moving the entire song up or down in pitch. To play songs in new keys, you'll need to learn more chords. Below are two Jam Cards you can use to learn new chords:

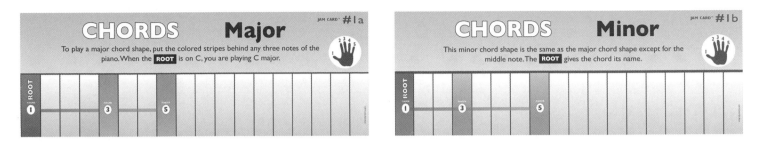

Place the root bar behind the root note of your chord, and the other shaded bars will show you which notes to use to play that chord:

Guitarists typically like to play in keys such as G, D, and A, whereas brass players often favor keys such as F, B♭, and E♭. By using your Jam Cards on the piano, all chords are easily accessible.

Here is the same chord progression in three different keys. Use the Jam Card to learn any chords you don't already know.

🎵 BEST DAY OF MY LIFE 🔊
American Authors

Here's the original key:

Here's the same song, transposed to a key that brass players might prefer:

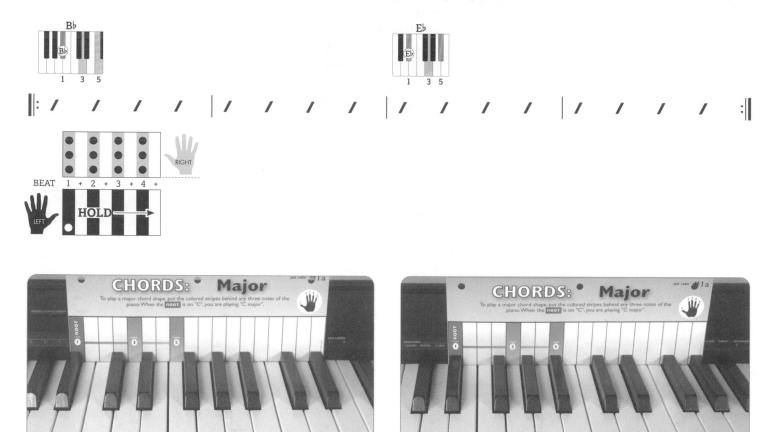

And here's a key for singers who may want to transpose it down, making it more comfortable to sing:

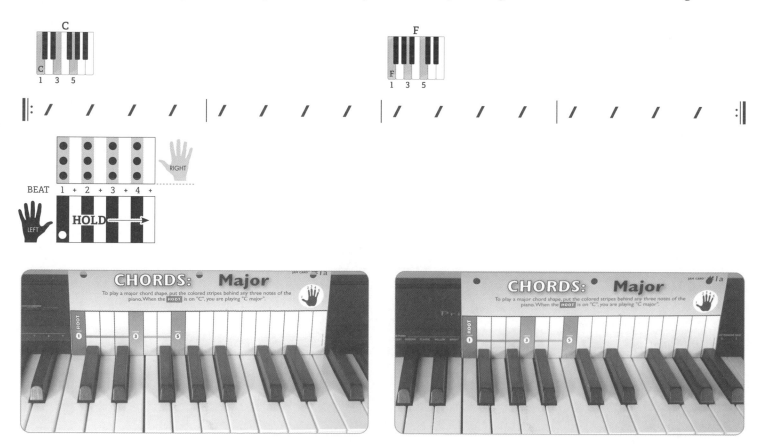

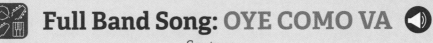
Form of Recording: Intro–Verse–Breakdown 1–Verse–Breakdown 1–Verse–Breakdown 1–
Verse–Breakdown 2–Verse

Here's the main keyboard riff:

Verse

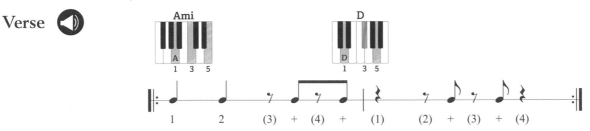

Here's the keyboard breakdown that happens periodically throughout "Oye Como Va." You can hear it first at the 0:30 mark of the original recording. Sometimes when this rhythm figure is played, you only play the first two bars:

Breakdown 1

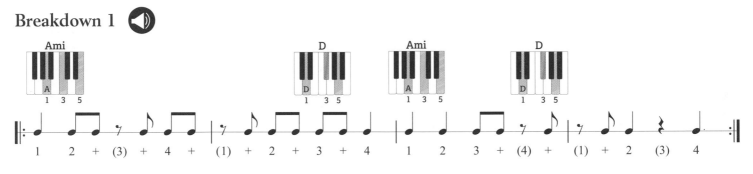

Here's the last section, which is played over an E chord. As before, the main riff alternates with this section in the Jam Track.

Breakdown 2

VERSE

Ami   D
Oye como va, mi ritmo.

Ami   D
Bueno pa gozar, mulata.

Ami   D
Oye como va, mi ritmo.

Ami   D
Bueno pa gozar, mulata.

SECTION 8

Music Theory: Melodic Note Reading

One way to keep practicing your reading is to learn more riffs. With these riffs, you can focus on some new rhythmic concepts. This song has rhythms we haven't yet read in this book. However, you can use your ear to listen to the song to learn the rhythms.

BURN
Ellie Goulding

This example has many notes played on the upbeats. We've added counting underneath the notes:

PUSH IT
Salt-N-Pepa

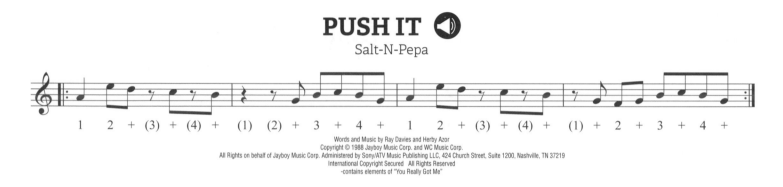

Music Theory: Syncopated Patterns

Here is a new comping pattern with syncopation; the Jam Track features only a drumbeat:

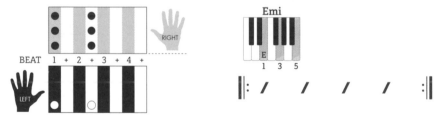

If you take that same comping pattern but change the chords (two chords per bar), then you can play some other songs:

HELLO
Adele

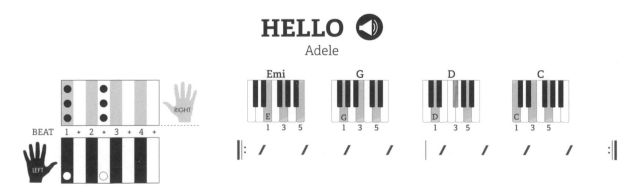

SEE YOU AGAIN

Wiz Khalifa ft. Charlie Puth

This last song features a **reggae** pattern; the Jam Track includes only drums for you to play with:

WAITING IN VAIN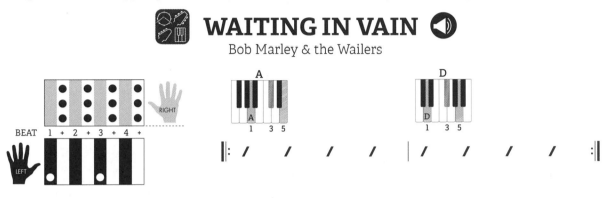

Bob Marley & the Wailers

Notice that the left hand always plays on beats 1 and 3 while the right hand plays on the upbeats.

Full Band Song: WAKA WAKA (THIS TIME FOR AFRICA)

Shakira

Form of Recording: Intro–Verse–Pre-Chorus–Chorus–Interlude–Verse–Pre-Chorus–Chorus–Bridge–Chorus

Every section of this song uses the same chord progression (save for the Bridge), and through most of the recording, the keyboard player outlines the chords with whole notes. To expand this performance, you can change the tones on the keyboard in different sections or play the chords in different **registers** (using higher or lower notes).

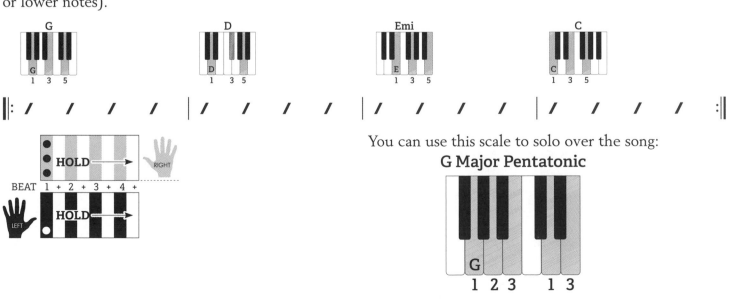

You can use this scale to solo over the song:

G Major Pentatonic

Words and Music by Shakira, Zolani Mahola, John Hill, Eugene Victor Doo Belley, Jean Ze Bella and Emile Kojidie
Copyright © 2010 Sony/ATV Music Publishing LLC, MyMPM Music, Freshly Ground, EMI April Music Inc., RodeoMan Music and Sony/ATV Music Publishing (Germany) Gmbh
All Rights Administered by Sony/ATV Music Publishing LLC, 424 Church Street, Suite 1200, Nashville, TN 37219
International Copyright Secured   All Rights Reserved

VERSE

G   D
You're a good soldier, choosing your battles.

     Emi   C
Pick yourself up and dust yourself off and get back in the saddle.

G   D
You're on the front line, everyone's watching.

     Emi   C
You know it's serious, we're getting closer, this isn't over.

G   D   Emi   C
The pressure's on, you feel it. But you got it all, believe it.

PRE-CHORUS

G   D
When you fall get up, oh, oh. And if you fall get up, eh, eh.

     Emi   C
Tsamina mina zangalewa, 'cause this is Africa.

CHORUS

G   D   Emi   C
Tsamina mina, eh, eh. Waka waka, eh, eh. Tsamina mina zangalewa, this time for Africa.

VERSE

G   D   Emi
Listen to your God. This is our motto. Your time to shine,

           C
don't wait in line, y vamos por todo.

G   D   Emi
People are raising their expectations. Go on and feed them,

           C
this is your moment, no hesitation.

G   D   Emi   C
Today's your day, I feel it. You paved the way, believe it.

PRE-CHORUS

G   D
If you get down get up, oh, oh. When you get down get up, eh, eh.

     Emi   C
Tsamina mina zangalewa, this time for Africa.

BRIDGE

G
Awabuye lamajoni, ipikipiki mama wa A to Z.

Bathi susa lamajoni, ipikipiki mama from East to West.

Bathi waka waka ma eh eh,

Waka waka ma eh eh,

Zonk' izizwe mazibuye, 'cause this is Africa.

SECTION 9

Music Theory: Notating Riffs

Play through this melody of "Little Talks" by Of Monsters and Men. The first four measures are written in notation. Write in the correct letter name above the rhythms:

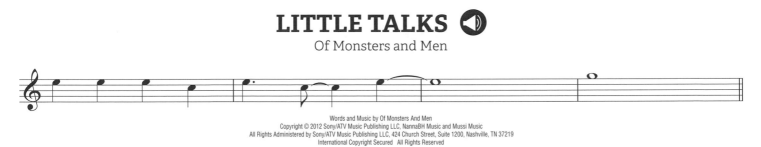

LITTLE TALKS
Of Monsters and Men

In that last example, we added a new type of rhythm: the **dotted note**. The dot adds half the value of the note back to itself. In this case, the dotted quarter notes equal one and a half beats. The last four measures of this melody are written using note names and rhythms. Rewrite the melody in the staff below:

Music Theory: Inversions

So far, when you've played chords on the piano, you have used three notes, and the lowest note has always been the note the chord is named after (the **root**). However, you can play those same three notes in a different order, and it would still be the same chord. Here is the C chord with C as its lowest note:

C

You can **invert** the C chord by taking the C note up an **octave** (same note name in a different spot on the keyboard). This shape is called **1st inversion**, reading E–G–C, from left to right:

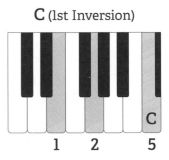

C (1st Inversion)

You can do this one more time by moving the E up an octave, ending up with the **2nd inversion** shape, reading G–C–E, from left to right:

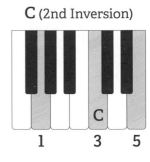

C (2nd Inversion)

Typically, the left hand will stay on the same root note, or the note the chord is named after, while the right hand plays an inversion. Apply inversions to the progression below. Here is a progression with the chords in root position:

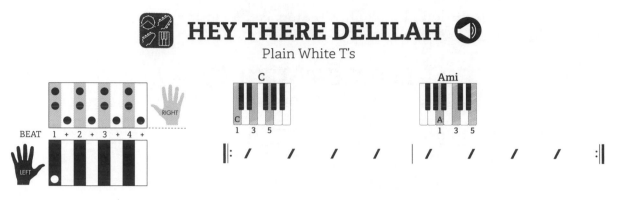

Try moving from a C chord to an Ami in 1st inversion. Note how two of the notes stay in the same place between chords:

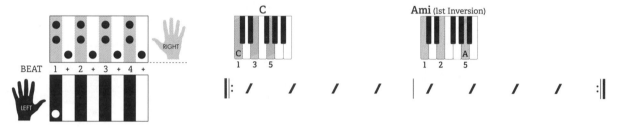

In this next example, do the same thing with a G to Emi progression, starting with the G chord in root position:

Next, try moving from a G to an Emi in 1st inversion. Note how two of the notes stay in the same place between chords:

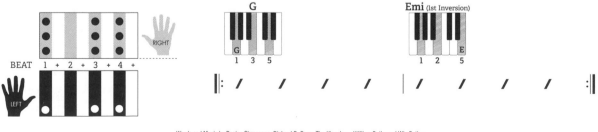

You can use different combinations of inversions and comping patterns for any song. Many professional keyboard players will use different inversions all the time, improvising which ones they want to use on the spot.

The following examples feature a common progression in popular music, giving you an opportunity to move around the keyboard with inversions.

Play the G chord on beats one and two, and then by beat 3, move to C and play "+ 4." Try it first in root position, and then play it with some inversions. Here are all the chords in root position:

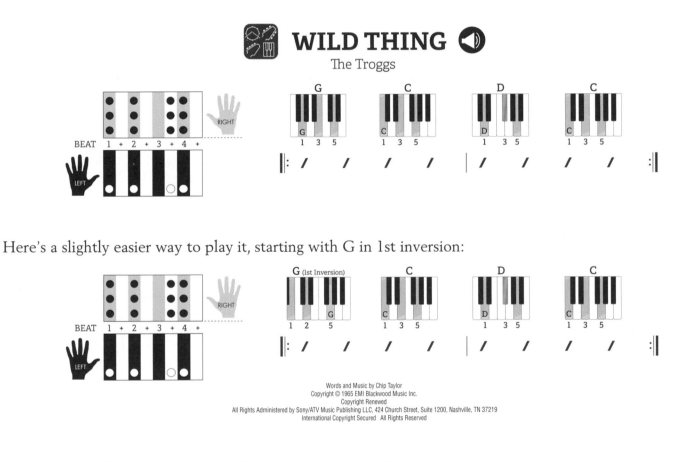

Below is one of the most common chord progressions in all of popular music:

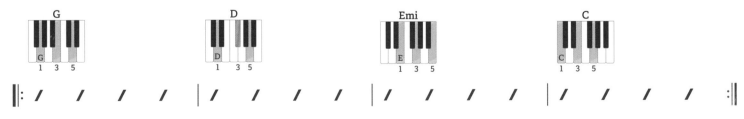

This progression can be found in many songs from the last 60 years, including: "Where Is the Love?" "Bored to Death," "Demons," "Apologize," "The Edge of Glory," "Trouble," "Someone Like You," "Poker Face," and hundreds of others. Try it with the Chorus of the pop song "The Edge of Glory" by Lady Gaga:

Composition: Verse and Chorus

Now that you know more chords, you can use them to compose songs. Create a new four-chord verse and chorus, using any of these seven chords you have already learned (A, Ami, C, D, E, Emi, G). Try using a syncopated rhythm for either the verse or chorus.

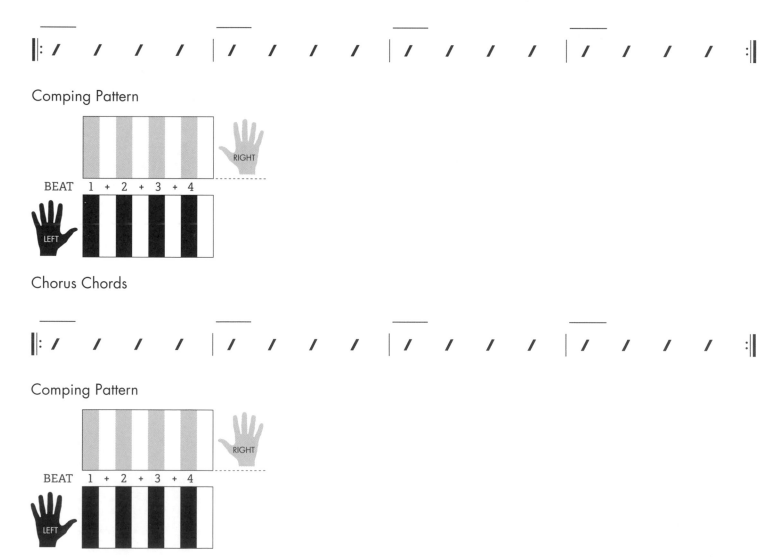

40

Improvisation: Comparing Major and Minor Pentatonic Scales

The major pentatonic scale looks a lot like the minor pentatonic scale. These two scales actually have the exact same notes (A, C, D, E, G). The only difference between the two scales (for now) is which note feels like home, or which is the **tonic**.

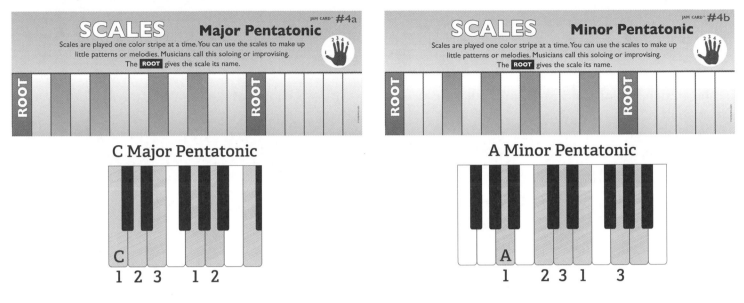

The notes in these two scales are exactly the same. The root is just on a different tonic note.

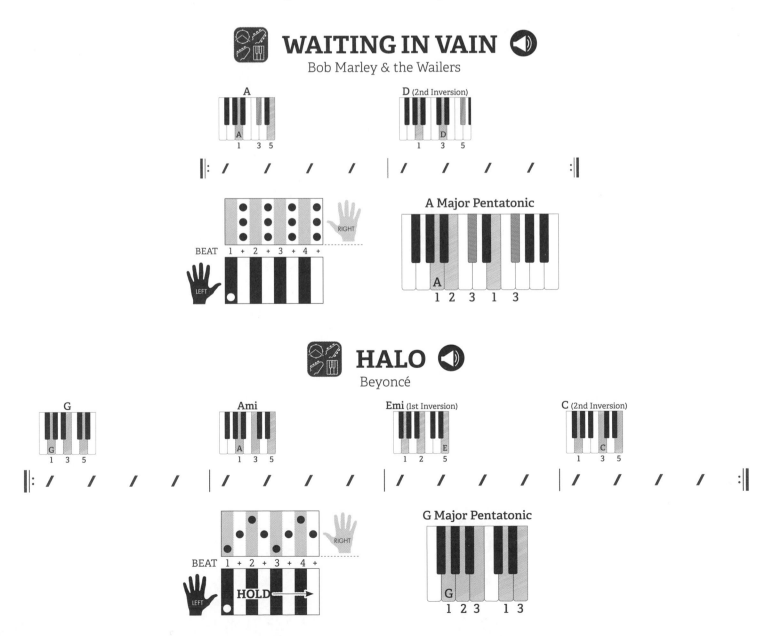

Full Band Song: BEST DAY OF MY LIFE
American Authors

Form of Recording: Intro–Verse–Pre-Chorus–Chorus–Verse–Pre-Chorus–Chorus–Bridge–Chorus

Intro Riff

In the fourth bar of the Pre-Chorus, there is a measure with no chord. Make sure to not play during that measure of music.

Chord Progressions

Verse/Chorus

Pre-Chorus

Bridge

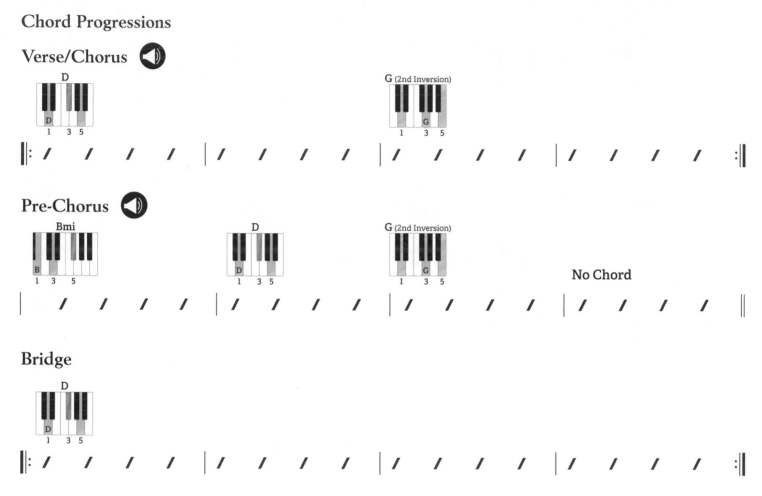

This song doesn't have a dedicated keyboard solo, but it's in the key of D major, so you can use the D major pentatonic scale to solo. Throw a keyboard solo in at the end over the last Chorus!

D Major Pentatonic

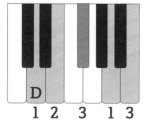

VERSE

D
I had a dream so big and loud. I jumped so high I touched the clouds.

G
Whoa-o-o-o-o-oh. Whoa-o-o-o-o-oh.

D
I stretched my hands out to the sky. We danced with monsters through the night.

G
Whoa-o-o-o-o-oh. Whoa-o-o-o-o-oh.

PRE-CHORUS

D   Emi
I'm never gonna look back, whoa. I'm never gonna give it up, no. Please don't wake me now.

CHORUS

D   G
Wo-o-o-o-oo! This is gonna be the best day of my life, my life.

D   G
Wo-o-o-o-oo! This is gonna be the best day of my life, my life.

VERSE

D
I howled at the moon with friends. And then the sun came crashing in.

G
Whoa-o-o-o-o-oh. Whoa-o-o-o-o-oh.

        D
But all the possibilities, no limits just epiphanies.

G
Whoa-o-o-o-o-oh. Whoa-o-o-o-o-oh.

BRIDGE

D
I hear it calling outside my window.

I feel it in my soul, soul.

The stars were burning so bright,

The sun was out 'til midnight.

I say we lose control, control.

SECTION 10

Music Theory: A Pentatonic Melody

Here is an example of a melody that uses the pentatonic scale:

SHAKE IT OFF
Taylor Swift

Music Theory: Ledger Lines and Bass Clef

Here is a pentatonic riff from "Closer" by the Chainsmokers. In this first example, play it using only staff notation:

CLOSER
The Chainsmokers ft. Halsey

This sounds higher than the recording, so you can play it down an octave. However, by moving it down an octave, it doesn't fit on the staff, so you'll need to use **ledger lines**. Ledger lines are used to extend the staff with more lines and spaces. Here is what it would look like starting on **middle C**, or the C that lies in the middle of the keyboard:

But perhaps you want to play this with even lower notes, in which case this would be written in the **bass clef**: 𝄢. The piano is one of the few instruments with a range wide enough to play very low and very high notes, and all those notes can be shown using two clefs and staves, one for lower notes (bass clef) and one for higher notes (treble clef). These two clefs are connected by the middle C:

Here are the notes of the bass clef:

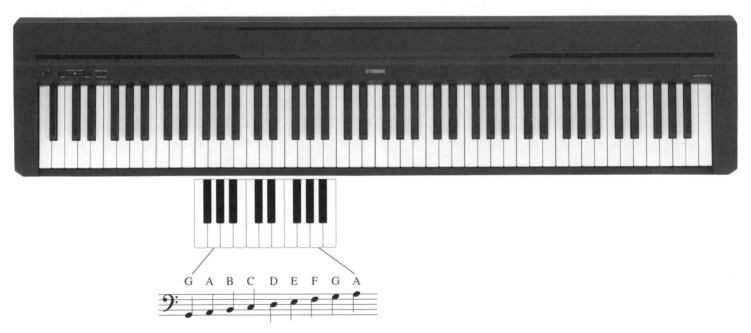

And here's the melody for "Closer" written in the bass clef, starting on the note C:

We will use both clefs a lot more in the future, but for now, just keep in mind that knowing them is another way to be a fluent musician at the keyboard.

Instrument Technique: Playing Bass Lines

We have now introduced the concept of bass clef reading, but how does it relate to the piano itself? For the most part, we have treated the left hand on the piano as part of the comping patterns, but sometimes it can be used to create more interesting and memorable bass lines.

Here are a few examples to try out. First, just play the bass line with your left hand, and then try playing the chords above in your right hand, with whole notes:

HAITI
Arcade Fire

UPTOWN FUNK
Mark Ronson feat. Bruno Mars

Full Band Song: KICK, PUSH
Lupe Fiasco

Form of Recording: Verse–Chorus–Verse–Chorus–Verse–Chorus

Main Keyboard Part

The last two measures of this figure show a bold, wavy line next to the half-note chords. This simply means to play each note separately and let them ring together. (These chords are new and different, but they will be covered in more detail in later books.)

* These notes are played at the same time.

VERSE

First got it when he was six, didn't know any tricks. Matter fact,

First time he got on it he slipped, landed on his hip and bust his lip.

For a week he had to talk with a lisp, like this.

Now we can end the story right here,

But shorty didn't quit, it was something in the air, yea.

He said it was somethin' so appealing. He couldn't fight the feelin'.

Somethin' about it, he knew he couldn't doubt it, couldn't understand it,

Brand it, since the first kickflip he landed, uh. Labeled a misfit, abandoned,

Ca-kunk, ca-kunk, kunk. His neighbors couldn't stand it, so he was banished to the park.

Started in the morning, wouldn't stop till after dark, yea.

When they said "it's getting late in here, so I'm sorry young man, there's no skating here."

CHORUS

So we kick, push, kick, push, kick, push, kick, push, coast.

And the way he roll just a rebel to the world with no place to go.

So we kick, push, kick, push, kick, push, kick, push, coast.

So come and skate with me, just a rebel looking for a place to be.

So let's kick, and push, and coast.

VERSE

Uh, uh, uh. My man got a lil' older, became a better roller (yea).

No helmet, hell-bent on killin' himself, was what his momma said.

But he was feelin' himself, got a lil' more swagger in his style.

Met his girlfriend, she was clappin' in the crowd.

Love is what was happening to him now, uh. He said "I would marry you but I'm engaged
to These aerials and varials, and I don't think this board is strong enough to carry two."

She said "beau, I weigh 120 pounds. Now, lemme make one thing clear, I don't need to ride

yours, I got mine right here." So she took him to a spot he didn't know about,

Somewhere in the apartment parking lot, she said, "I don't normally take dates in here."

Security came and said, "I'm sorry there's no skating here."

CHORUS

So they kick, push, kick, push, kick, push, kick, push, coast.

And the way they roll, just lovers intertwined with no place to go.

And so they kick, push, kick, push, kick, push, kick, push, coast.

So come and skate with me, just a rebel looking for a place to be.

So let's kick, and push, and coast.

VERSE

Yea uh, yea, yea. Before he knew he had a crew that wasn't no punk

In they Spitfire shirts and SB Dunks. They would push, till they couldn't skate no more.

Office buildings, lobbies wasn't safe no more.

And it wasn't like they wasn't getting chased no more,

Just the freedom is better than breathing, they said.

An escape route, they used to escape out when things got crazy they needed to break out.

(They'd head) to any place with stairs, and good grinds the world was theirs, uh.

And they four wheels would take them there,

Until the cops came and said, "There's no skating here."

CHORUS

So they kick, push, kick, push, kick, push, kick, push, coast.

And the way they roll, just rebels without a cause with no place to go.

And so they kick, push, kick, push, kick, push, kick, push, coast.

So come roll with me, just a rebel looking for a place to be.

So let's kick, and push, and coast.

SECTION 11

Music Theory: The Blues Scale

Both of these riffs use the **blues scale**; it simply adds a passing note between the third and fourth notes of the minor pentatonic scale:

BAD
Michael Jackson

SUNSHINE OF YOUR LOVE
Cream

Here is the blues scale on a Jam Card:

Try this scale with this next song, which also uses the Dmi chord from the last section:

EVIL WAYS
Santana

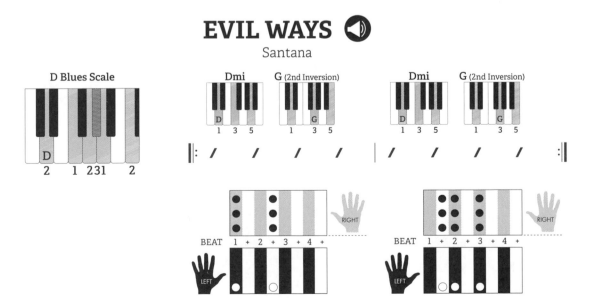

49

Music Theory: Common Tones ▶

Look at the chord progression C–Ami, which is used in the Intro to "Hey There Delilah":

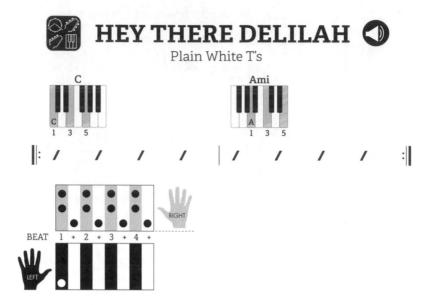

What are the notes in each chord? Answer: **C–E–G** and **A–C–E**. Now, which notes are in common? Answer: C and E, which are called **common tones**. To move easily between chords, keep the common tones and only move the changing note. You can play these three different ways:

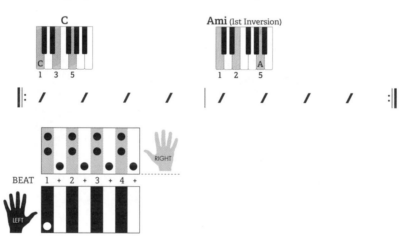

You may find that starting with an inverted chord is the easiest way to play a progression:

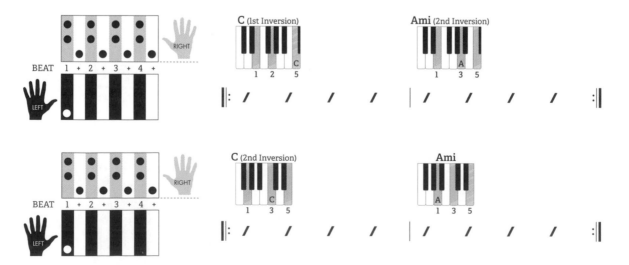

Try playing the root of each chord with your left hand while playing the inverted chords with your right:

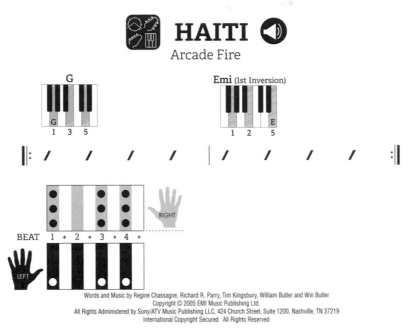

Composition: Composing with Inversions

Now it's your turn to make up a song based on inversions:

1. Using this Jam Card, choose four chords, in any key you'd like. We've picked D, Bmi, G, and Emi in the key of D as an example:

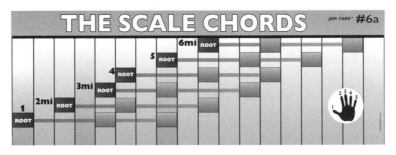

2. Write the notes of each chord above the chord name, and then figure out the common tones between them:

    D: D–F♯–A
    Bmi: B–D–F♯
    G: G–B–D
    Emi: E–G–D

 shares D and F♯ with

shares D and B with

shares G and B with

3. Write in the inversions you could use that keep the most common tones from chord to chord. Here is an example solution:

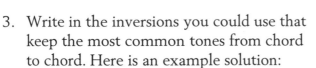

Full Band Song: UMBRELLA

Rihanna

Form of Recording: Intro–Verse–Chorus–Verse–Chorus–Bridge–Chorus

Verse

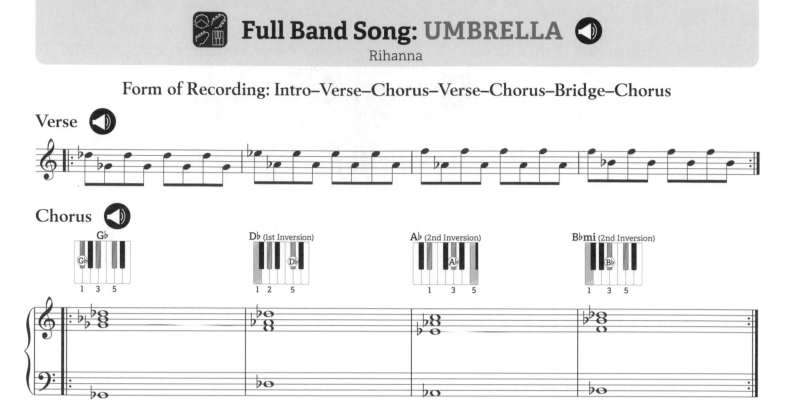

Chorus

Verse 2

Material is often repeated in music, but with different endings. To show this, we write **first** and **second endings**. These are the measures in the staff labeled **1** and **2**. To play this, perform the first four measures and then repeat. Then, when playing it the second time, skip the first ending and play the second ending. This verse also uses **power chords**. Power chords are chords that have only a root and 5th, no 3rd.

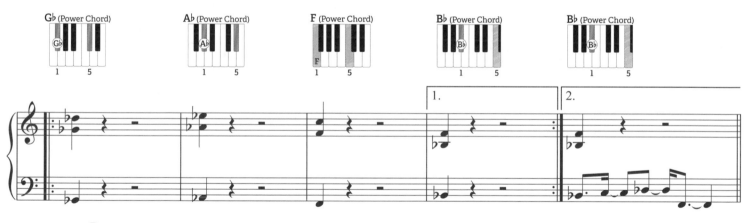

Bridge

The Bridge features a chord that can cause some confusion, but don't worry, it's easy to understand! The first chord of the bridge is Cb, and you might be wondering: "Why not call this a B major chord?" This is because this particular chord has to be labeled as a Cb major chord according to music theory rules, which we will cover more in the next book.

The Bridge also has a first and second ending. Play the four measures before the repeat sign the first time, and then during the second time, skip measure 4 and move to the second ending:

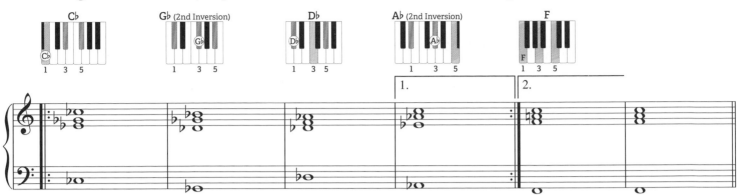

You can use the B♭ blues scale to solo:

B♭ Blues Scale

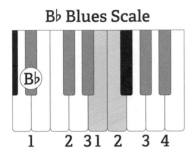

VERSE

    G♭5   **A♭5**
You have my heart, and we'll never be worlds apart.

        F5   **B♭5**
Maybe in magazines, but you'll still be my star.

        G♭5   **A♭5**
Baby, 'cause in the dark you can't see shiny cars.

        F5   **B♭5**
And that's when you need me there, with you I'll always share, because...

CHORUS

G♭   **D♭**   **A♭**
When the sun shines, we'll shine together. Told you I'd be here forever.

        B♭
Said I'll always be your friend. Took an oath, I'mma stick it out 'til the end.

G♭   **D♭**   **A♭**
Now that it's raining more than ever, know that we'll still have each other.

        B♭   **G♭**
You can stand under my umbrella. You can stand under my umbrella.

    D♭   **A♭**
(Ella, ella, eh, eh, eh.) Under my umbrella.

    B♭   **G♭**
(Ella, ella, eh, eh, eh.) Under my umbrella.

    D♭   **A♭**
(Ella, ella, eh, eh, eh.) Under my umbrella.

    B♭
(Ella, ella, eh, eh, eh, eh, eh, eh.)

VERSE

          G♭5   A♭5
These fancy things, will never come in between.

              F5   B♭5
You're part of my entity, here for infinity.

          G♭5   A♭5
When the war has took its part, when the world has dealt its cards,

     F5   B♭5
If the hand is hard, together we'll mend your heart.

BRIDGE

C♭   G♭
You can run into my arms. It's OK, don't be alarmed.

         D♭   A♭
Come here to me. There's no distance in between our love.

C♭   G♭
So go on and let the rain pour.

                         F
I'll be all you need and more, because...

SECTION 12

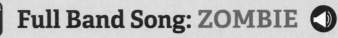

Full Band Song: ZOMBIE
The Cranberries

Form of Recording: Intro–Verse–Chorus–Verse–Chorus–Bridge/Outro

Note that during the Chorus, we recommend using power chords instead of full triads.

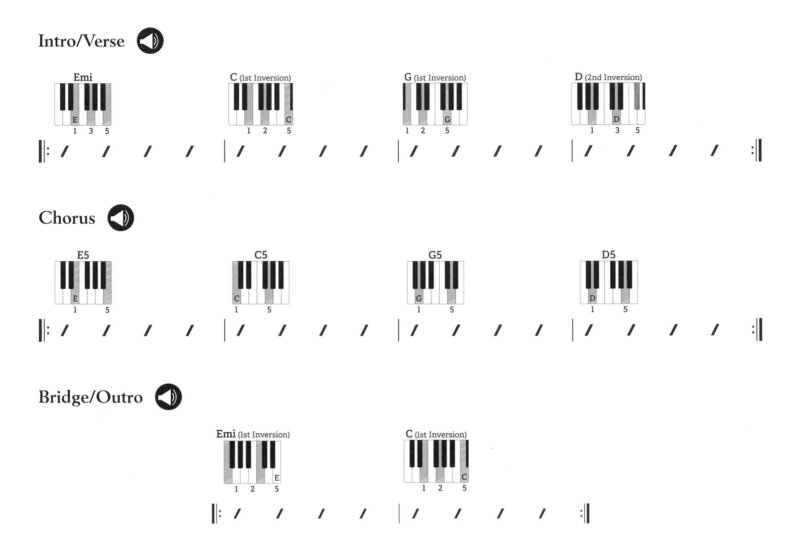

There is only one more section needed—the simple guitar riff at the end of the Chorus, which we can also play on piano:

VERSE

Emi   C   G   D

Another head hangs lowly, child is slowly taken.

Emi   C   G   D

And the violence caused such silence. Who are we mistaken?

              Emi   C   G   D

But you see it's not me, it's not my family. In your head, in your head they are fighting,

              Emi   C

With their tanks, and their bombs, and their bombs, and their guns.

            G   D

In your head, in your head they are crying.

CHORUS

        E5   C5   G5   D5

In your head, in your head, zombie, zombie, zombie, hey, hey.

              E5   C5   G5   D5

What's in your head, in your head, zombie, zombie, zombie, hey, hey, hey?

VERSE

Emi   C   G   D

Another mother's breakin' heart is taking over.

Emi   C   G   D

When the violence causes silence, we must be mistaken.

              Emi   C   G   D

It's the same old theme since nineteen-sixteen. In your head, in your head they're still fighting,

              Emi   C

With their tanks, and their bombs, and their bombs, and their guns.

              G   D

In your head, in your head they are dying.

CHORUS

        E5   C5   G5   D5

In your head, in your head, zombie, zombie, zombie, hey, hey.

              E5   C5   G5   D5

What's in your head, in your head, zombie, zombie, zombie. Hey, hey, hey?

Please laminate each Jam Card after removing it from the book.

JAM CARD™ #1a

CHORDS

Major

To play a major chord shape, put the colored stripes behind any three notes of the piano. When the **ROOT** is on C, you are playing C major.

FINGER **5**

FINGER **3**

THUMB **1**
ROOT

JAM CARD™ #1b

CHORDS

Minor

This minor chord shape is the same as the major chord shape except for the middle note. The **ROOT** gives the chord its name.

FINGER **5**

FINGER **3**

THUMB **1**
ROOT

Please laminate each Jam Card after removing it from the book.

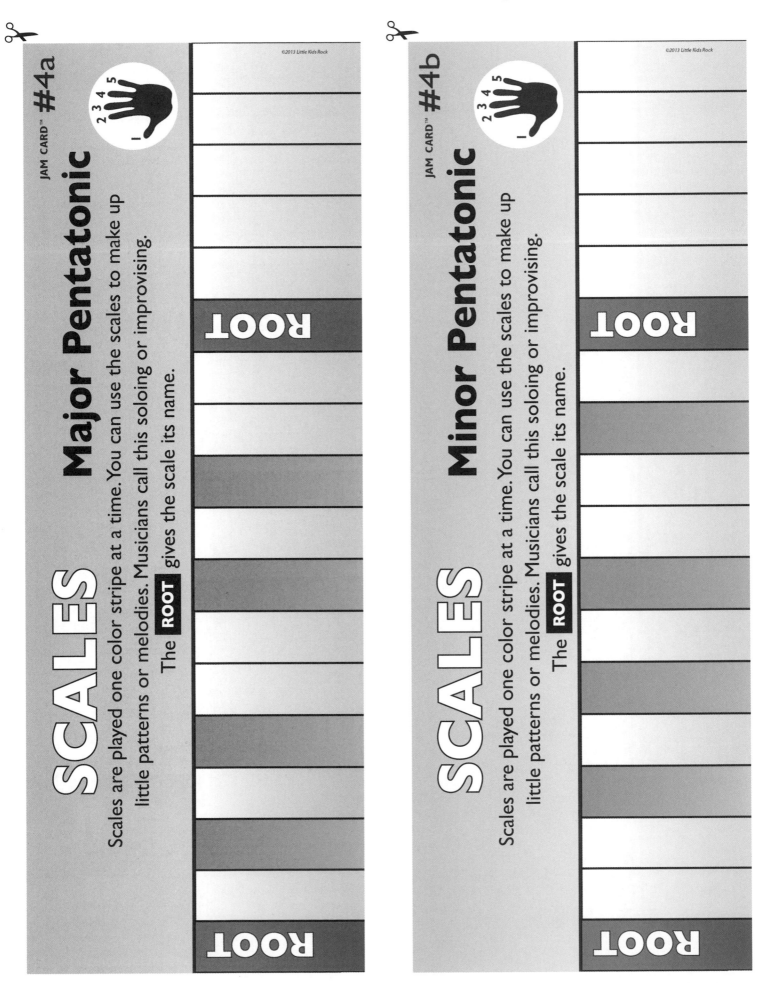

JAM CARD™ #4a

SCALES
Major Pentatonic

Scales are played one color stripe at a time. You can use the scales to make up little patterns or melodies. Musicians call this soloing or improvising. The **ROOT** gives the scale its name.

ROOT

ROOT

JAM CARD™ #4b

SCALES
Minor Pentatonic

Scales are played one color stripe at a time. You can use the scales to make up little patterns or melodies. Musicians call this soloing or improvising. The **ROOT** gives the scale its name.

ROOT

ROOT

Please laminate each Jam Card after removing it from the book.

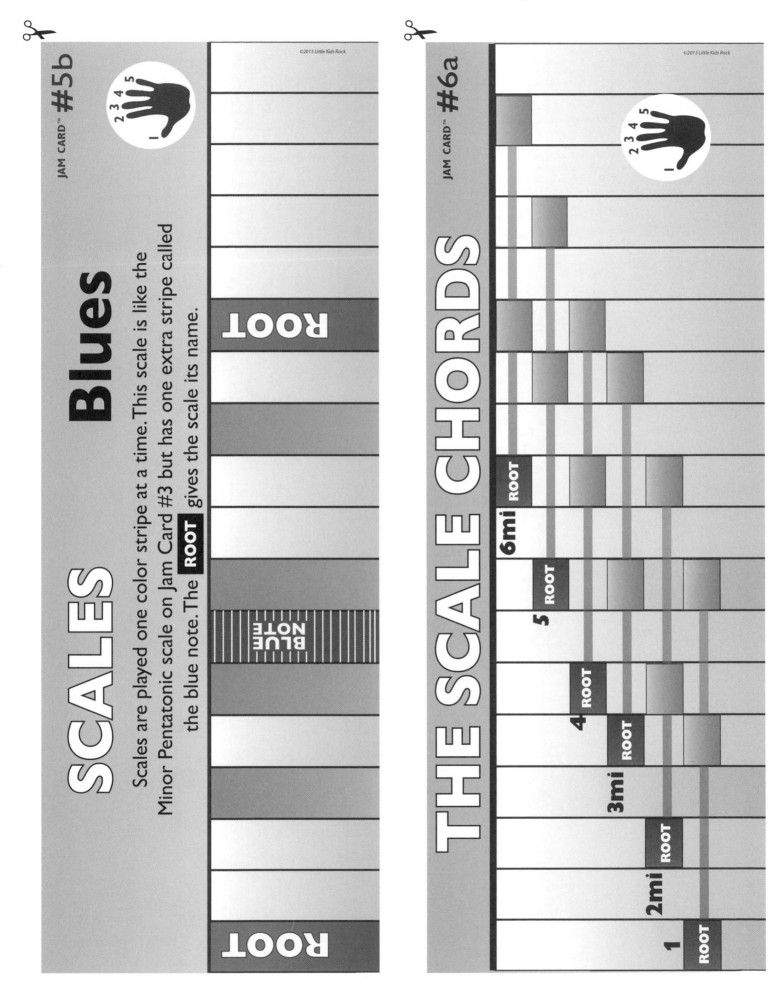

JAM CARD™ #5b

SCALES

Blues

Scales are played one color stripe at a time. This scale is like the Minor Pentatonic scale on Jam Card #3 but has one extra stripe called the blue note. The ROOT gives the scale its name.

ROOT

ROOT

BLUE NOTE

ROOT

©2013 Little Kids Rock

JAM CARD™ #6a

THE SCALE CHORDS

1
ROOT

2mi
ROOT

3mi
ROOT

4
ROOT

5
ROOT

6mi
ROOT

©2013 Little Kids Rock

HAL•LEONARD KEYBOARD PLAY-ALONG

AUDIO ACCESS INCLUDED

The **Keyboard Play-Along** series will help you quickly and easily play your favorite songs as played by your favorite artists. Just follow the music in the book, listen to the audio to hear how the keyboard should sound, and then play along using the separate backing tracks. The melody and lyrics are also included in the book in case you want to sing, or simply to help you follow along. The audio files are enhanced so you can adjust the recording to any tempo without changing pitch! Each book/audio pack in this series features eight great songs.

1. POP/ROCK HITS

Against All Odds (Take a Look at Me Now) • Deacon Blues • (Everything I Do) I Do It for You • Hard to Say I'm Sorry • Kiss on My List • My Life • Walking in Memphis • What a Fool Believes.
00699875 Keyboard Transcriptions $14.95

2. SOFT ROCK

Don't Know Much • Glory of Love • I Write the Songs • It's Too Late • Just Once • Making Love Out of Nothing at All • We've Only Just Begun • You Are the Sunshine of My Life.
00699876 Keyboard Transcriptions $14.95

3. CLASSIC ROCK

Against the Wind • Come Sail Away • Don't Do Me like That • Jessica • Say You Love Me • Takin' Care of Business • Werewolves of London • You're My Best Friend.
00699877 Keyboard Transcriptions $14.95

6. ROCK BALLADS

Bridge over Troubled Water • Easy • Hey Jude • Imagine • Maybe I'm Amazed • A Whiter Shade of Pale • You Are So Beautiful • Your Song.
00699880 Keyboard Transcriptions $17.99

7. ROCK CLASSICS

Baba O'Riley • Bloody Well Right • Carry on Wayward Son • Changes • Cold As Ice • Evil Woman • Space Truckin' • That's All.
00699881 Keyboard Transcriptions $14.95

9. ELTON JOHN BALLADS

Blue Eyes • Candle in the Wind • Daniel • Don't Let the Sun Go Down on Me • Goodbye Yellow Brick Road • Rocket Man (I Think It's Gonna Be a Long Long Time) • Someone Saved My Life Tonight • Sorry Seems to Be the Hardest Word.
00700752 Keyboard Transcriptions $14.99

10. STEELY DAN

Aja • Do It Again • FM • Hey Nineteen • Peg • Reeling in the Years • Rikki Don't Lose That Number.
00700201 Keyboard Transcriptions $14.99

13. BILLY JOEL – HITS

Allentown • Just the Way You Are • New York State of Mind • Pressure • Root Beer Rag • Scenes from an Italian Restaurant • She's Always a Woman • Tell Her About It.
00700303 Keyboard Transcriptions $14.99

16. 1970s Rock

Dream On • Highway Star • I Feel the Earth Move • Foreplay/Long Time (Long Time) • Point of Know Return • Sweet Home Alabama • Take the Long Way Home • Will It Go Round in Circles.
00700933 Keyboard Transcriptions $14.99

17. 1960s ROCK

Gimme Some Lovin' • Green Onions • I'm a Believer • Louie, Louie • Magic Carpet Ride • Oh, Pretty Woman • Runaway • The Twist.
00700935 Keyboard Transcriptions $14.99

18. 1950s ROCK

Blueberry Hill • Good Golly Miss Molly • Great Balls of Fire • The Great Pretender • Rock and Roll Is Here to Stay • Shake, Rattle and Roll • Tutti Frutti • What'd I Say.
00700934 Keyboard Transcriptions $14.99

19. JAZZ CLASSICS

Blues Etude • (They Long to Be) Close to You • Freeway • Lonely Woman • My Foolish Heart • Tin Tin Deo • Watch What Happens.
00701244 Keyboard Transcriptions $14.99

20. STEVIE WONDER

Boogie On Reggae Woman • Higher Ground • I Wish • Isn't She Lovely • Living for the City • Sir Duke • Superstition • You Are the Sunshine of My Life.
00701262 Keyboard Transcriptions $14.99

22. CAROLE KING

I Feel the Earth Move • It's Too Late • Jazzman • (You Make Me Feel Like) a Natural Woman • So Far Away • Sweet Seasons • Will You Love Me Tomorrow (Will You Still Love Me Tomorrow) • You've Got a Friend.
00701756 Keyboard Transcriptions $17.99

24. DREAM THEATER

Breaking All Illusions • Erotomania • Fatal Tragedy • Hell's Kitchen • In the Presence of Enemies - Part 1 • Metropolis-Part 1 "The Miracle and the Sleeper" • On the Backs of Angels • Six Degrees of Inner Turbulence: I. Overture • Six Degrees of Inner Turbulence: II. About to Crash • Under a Glass Moon.
00111941 Keyboard Transcriptions $24.99

HAL•LEONARD®
www.halleonard.com

Prices, contents, and availability subject to change without notice.

FIRST 50 SONGS
YOU SHOULD PLAY ON THE PIANO

*You've been taking lessons, you've got a few chords under your belt, and you're ready to buy a songbook. Now what? Hal Leonard has the answers in its **First 50** series.*

These books contain easy to intermediate arrangements with lyrics for must-know songs. Each arrangement is simple and streamlined, yet still captures the essence of the tune.

3-Chord Songs
00249666.............................$19.99

4-Chord Songs
00249562.............................$17.99

Acoustic Songs
00293416.............................$17.99

Baroque Pieces
00291453.............................$15.99

Blues Songs
00293318.............................$16.99

Broadway Songs
00150167.............................$17.99

Christmas Carols
00147216.............................$15.99

Christmas Songs
00172041.............................$15.99

Classic Rock
00195619.............................$17.99

Classical Pieces
00131436.............................$15.99

Country Songs
00150166.............................$16.99

Disney Songs
00274938.............................$22.99

Duets
00276571.............................$24.99

Early Rock Songs
00160570.............................$15.99

Folk Songs
00235867.............................$15.99

Fun Children's Songs
00355369.............................$16.99

Gospel Songs
00282526.............................$15.99

Hymns
00275199.............................$15.99

Jazz Classics
00363096.............................$16.99

Jazz Standards
00196269.............................$15.99

Kids' Songs
00196071.............................$15.99

Latin Songs
00248747.............................$17.99

Love Ballads
00457002.............................$19.99

Movie Songs
00150165.............................$17.99

Movie Themes
00278368.............................$17.99

Piano Solos
00365906.............................$17.99

Pop Ballads
00248987.............................$19.99

Pop Hits
00234374.............................$19.99

Popular Songs
00131140.............................$17.99

R&B Songs
00196028.............................$17.99

Relaxing Songs
00327506 ....$17.99

Rock Songs
00195619.............................$17.99

TV Themes
00294319.............................$15.99

Worship Songs
00287138.............................$19.99

HAL•LEONARD®
www.halleonard.com

Prices, content and availability subject to change without notice.